THE LIBRARY OF HOLOCAUST TESTIMONIES

Trust and Deceit

The Library of Holocaust Testimonies

Editors: Antony Polonsky, Sir Martin Gilbert CBE, Aubrey Newman,
Raphael F. Scharf, Ben Helfgott MBE

Under the auspices of the Yad Vashem Committee of the Board of Deputies of
British Jews and the Centre for Holocaust Studies, University of Leicester

Trust and Deceit

A Tale of Survival in Slovakia and
Hungary, 1939–1945

GERTA VRBOVÁ

VALLENTINE MITCHELL
LONDON • PORTLAND, OR

First published in 2006 by
VALLENTINE MITCHELL

920 NE 58th Avenue, Suite 300
Portland, Oregon 97213-3786

Suite 314, Premier House
Edgware, Middlesex HA8 7BJ

www.vmbooks.com

Copyright © 2006 Gerta Vrbová
reprinted 2008

British Library Cataloguing in Publication Data

A catalogue record has been applied for

ISBN 978 0 85303 630 2

Library of Congress Cataloging-in-Publication Data

A catalogue record has been applied for

Printed by CPI Antony Rowe, Eastbourne, East Sussex

Contents

List of Plates

The Library of Holocaust Testimonies

Ten years have passed since Frank Cass launched his Library of Holocaust Testimonies. It was greatly to his credit that this was done, and even more remarkable that it has continued and flourished. The memoirs of each survivor throw new light and cast new perspectives on the fate of the Jews of Europe during the Holocaust. No voice is too small or humble to be heard, no story so familiar that it fails to tell the reader something new, something hitherto unnoticed, something previously unknown.

Each new memoir adds to our knowledge not only of the Holocaust, but also of many aspects of the human condition that are universal and timeless: the power of evil and the courage of the oppressed; the cruelty of the bystanders and the heroism of those who sought to help, despite the risks; the part played by family and community; the question of who knew what and when; the responsibility of the wider world for the destructive behaviour of tyrants and their henchmen.

Fifty memoirs are already in print in the Library of Holocaust Testimonies, and several more are being published each year. In this way anyone interested in the Holocaust will be able to draw upon a rich seam of eyewitness accounts. They can also use another Vallentine Mitchell publication, the multi-volume *Holocaust Memoir Digest*, edited by Esther Goldberg, to explore the contents of survivor memoirs in a way that makes them particularly accessible to teachers and students alike.

Sir Martin Gilbert
London, April 2005

To my oldest daughter,
Dr Helena Vrbová

Acknowledgements

First and foremost my thanks go to all those in Slovakia and Hungary who helped me to survive the war. Without their contribution to my survival this account could never have been written. I am immensely grateful to my parents and family whose affection and care during my early, formative years gave me the strength and desire to survive.

In more recent times, I owe my thanks to friends and colleagues who read early versions of my manuscript and persuaded me that my story is interesting, worthwhile to write down and publish. They include Professor Geoffrey Burnstock, Professor Tessa Gordon, Professor Olga Hudlická, Dr Anna Koffer, Dr Martin Rosendahl, Professor Robert Balázs, Dr Lilly Dubowitz, Geoffrey Hulme and Professor Ruth Bellairs. Without their encouragement I would have given up this project. Rowland Morgan and Leonora Klein had useful critical comments regarding the craft of writing and I hope that taking these to heart has somewhat helped to improve the quality of my writing. My thanks to Professor Rudolf Vrba (Walter), who checked my manuscript for accuracy and helped with his comments. I am particularly indebted to Professor Rudolf Klein, who tirelessly went through the whole manuscript and improved it wherever possible.

I tried not to burden my children Zuza Vrbová-Jackson, Caroline and Peter Hilton and grandchildren Hannah and Jan Janulewicz, Matthew and Zoë Hilton-Webb, Jack and Danny Hilton with my tale, but I could not entirely exclude them from telling them my wartime experiences. I am grateful for their patience and for helping me to persevere with my writing. Finally many thanks to Debbie Bartram for her help in preparing the manuscript and pointing out passages that were incomprehensible.

I apologize to those friends and colleagues whom I forgot to mention.

Introduction

I should like to explain why I now feel the need to extract from my memory people, places and events that have been buried there for half a century. After all, 'forgetting' them was what helped me to live a normal life, pursue my career as a scientist and bring up my children, with what I hope was minimal damage.

Yet the burden of my past, the memories of my loving family who perished in the gas chambers of Nazi Germany and the story of my survival are now haunting me and demanding that they be written down so that they should not be irretrievably lost. I owe those who did not survive the Holocaust, as well as those who might benefit from my experience, an account of my observations of certain events that took place in Europe during those terrible years when a highly sophisticated society perpetrated the most horrible crimes in history.

On my return home to Czechoslovakia, after the end of the war in May 1945, I made some sketchy notes of the events and my experiences between 1939 and 1945, just in case I might later forget them. I returned to these notes recently when I began to write the recollections of my life during this time. Very soon I realized that I did not need the notes. The events of those years were so indelibly etched in my memory that I could recall them in surprising, and often agonizing, detail. This ability to recall with clarity and precision my life during the dangerous years when I was fighting for survival suddenly failed me when I was attempting to remember the experiences I had after being liberated in Hungary by the Russians in January 1945. My recollections of the time between January and the start of my new life as a student of medicine in Prague in the autumn of 1945 were hazy, and lacked the vivid texture of those of previous years. Nevertheless I have included them in the biography, for they do form an integral part of the story. Maybe they also illustrate that the desire for survival and the intensity, determination and often ruthlessness that I employed in its pursuit during the years of acute danger influenced my personality much more then I had realized.

I was just 12 years old in 1939 and witnessed the changes around me that led to the destruction of Slovak Jews. Both the victims and their neighbours, who so willingly handed over their fellow citizens to be herded into cattle trucks and transported to their certain deaths, were skilfully manipulated by a complex and sophisticated bureaucracy into believing that such events were inevitable. With amazement and incomprehension I watched my family and most of my friends being rounded up without resistance or attempts to escape, because their social training had conditioned them to believe that in every society 'laws', however ruthless or obviously wicked, had to be obeyed.

I would like to recreate the atmosphere and interrelationships that existed within my own Jewish family and our love and respect for each other, which more than anything else helped me to grow up into an adult with much respect for life and little bitterness, in spite of my wartime experiences. I will try to describe how, as a child and later a teenager, I perceived the changes around me that destroyed our Jewish community and also to illustrate the loss of integrity and dignity of our Slovak, and later Hungarian, neighbours. Above all I would like finally to understand, and then convey, whatever insight I have gained into the question of how to survive in such adverse conditions. After all, at the ages of 16 and 17 I managed to avoid being rounded up and killed. Of course there is an element of luck in these matters, but chance plays only a small part and other things such as recognizing whom to 'trust' and whom to 'deceive' are much more important. It is of these I want to write.

1 Trnava, 1939–42

I remember a very special day when I allowed myself to believe that I belonged to my homeland, Slovakia. On my way home from school I always passed the Jesuit seminary. Perhaps it was because of the plaster crumbling from its ancient walls and the barred windows, grimy with centuries-old dirt that this sixteenth-century building, one of the oldest ones in Trnava, usually made me feel uncomfortable.

Yet on that day I was too happy for the sight of the building to spoil my mood. I was walking home with two of my friends, our schoolbags heavy with books. The reason for my elated mood was the fact that I had been chosen to be one of the pupils to read the poems of some of my favourite Slovak poets at parents' evening. And if this was not enough to fill me with joy, the teacher had also chosen one of my own poems to be read.

Even the cobbled, uneven stones under my shoes didn't annoy me as they usually did on my way home. As I reached our house I waved a cheerful 'Goodbye' to my friends and ran towards home.

The house stood tall in the marketplace. In the centre of the marketplace was a fountain and a statue of the holy trinity. All the surrounding houses faced the fountain.

I opened the heavy wooden gate, ran up the cool stone steps and burst into the upstairs flat that was my home, shared with my parents and grandma. I could smell immediately the delicious aroma of roast goose.

The first room that led off the entrance hall was a small

living room furnished with white cane furniture with a low table in the middle. I found my grandma in the kitchen, dressed as usual in a long black dress, her shiny brown hair tied in a bun. Her sparkling hazel eyes followed me as I entered the kitchen and gave her a big hug. She was getting my lunch ready, and looked very pleased with herself: 'What has happened? You look really happy.' I couldn't wait to tell her the news, and she smiled: 'I must have known this was a special day, for I cooked your favourite dish for you.' Now that she mentioned it, I realised that the roast goose I could smell as I entered the flat had been prepared specially for me. It was, indeed, my favourite meal. 'But how did you know?' Grandma looked at me, and said with a mischievous smile: 'Well, you said that the pupils who will read poetry at the parents evening would be chosen today. I knew how much you wanted to be among those chosen, and thought that if you were chosen, as I thought you would be, we should celebrate, and if not, a good meal would comfort you.' I gave her a special big kiss, and went out of the kitchen to search the flat to tell the great news to someone else. But, disappointingly, there was no one else there.

My father was probably trying to convert some of his fantasies into a successful business in the local coffee bar. This time his plans were connected with running our butcher's shop more efficiently, by implementing one of his crazy friend's inventions. They planned to design a room which would be well enough insulated (something like a giant Thermos flask), where, during the winter, cold air could be collected and then preserved and used to cool food during the summer. Unfortunately he had not trained as an engineer and was exploited by people he thought were professionals. His enthusiasm and trust in his friends cost us all our money. Only my mother's skills in business saved us from bankruptcy. She ran a very successful company in Bratislava, commuting every day and working long hours. I knew that she would not return until late at night, so I had to wait to share my news with my parents.

I went to my room and sat down at the desk trying to decide on the poems to read at the parents' evening. While thinking about this problem I looked at the cork board above my desk, where I pinned pieces of paper with aphorisms I thought I needed to remember and perhaps to follow. The day before, while browsing through my books, I had written out a new slogan that I had read in a translation of Dante's *Divine Comedy*. It greatly appealed to me and I thought it would help me to be independent. It read: 'Go your own way and let the people talk.'

By the time I had re-read it, and thought about it, Grandma called me for lunch. I had to hurry, she said, for after the meal she would be playing cards with Auntie Kate and Uncle Max. I was famished, and disposed of my lunch before the card game started. The roast goose was just right, the skin golden brown and crisp. I loved the stewed apple that Grandma always served with it. My mother would be angry that Grandma had spoiled me by cooking food specially for me, but Grandma considered me too skinny and frail and thought I needed feeding up.

Soon after we had finished lunch Uncle Max and Auntie Katie arrived, and the card game started.

Great-uncle Max was about 80, and had been a well-known criminal lawyer in Vienna, where he had defended many famous villains. Now he was partially deaf, with thick white hair, distinguished looks and a deep bossy voice. When I was about 11 years old and in the first class of our gymnasium, whenever Uncle Max visited us he talked to me in Latin, which I did not understand at all. These days Uncle Max lived in a farmhouse outside Trnava with one of my uncles, and was driven in a horse-drawn carriage to our house in Trnava to play cards with Auntie Kate and my grandmother, Jeanette. The three of them played at a card table covered with green fel, in the large room right under the picture of a distinguished ancestor of the family, Rabbi Simon Sidon. In the painting Rabbi Simon had a long, white beard and watched the card players with mistrustful eyes. He was indeed a distinguished

person, the first person in Trnava to introduce formal education, not only for Jewish children but for all children under
the age of 10. Nevertheless, here in our house, his supervision
didn't prevent Auntie Kate from cheating both her partners.

Kate was a small, wiry woman, with large, innocent-
looking blue eyes and long white hair which she wore in a
bun. She pretended to be completely deaf, and would place a
strange machine in front of her with a huge horn attached to
it, which was supposed to be a very modern hearing aid. This
instrument was switched on very seldom. Once I asked her:
'Auntie Kate, why don't you use your hearing aid? Don't you
want to know what people say?' Auntie Kate gave me a sly
look and said: 'You see, Gerti, it is much easier to assess what
people think or what hand they have when playing cards, if
one does not hear what they say, but only watches their faces.'
So I left it at that.

Most afternoons when the three old people settled down
to play cards, the same scene was re-enacted. Kate cheated,
and Max shouted into her hearing aid to protest against this
crime, not realizing that Kate heard nothing of the abuse.
Nevertheless Kate looked hurt and sad and pretended to be
really upset. My grandma would watch the scene with
amusement. Finally Max concluded: 'Look, Kate, it is impossible to play cards with you, and I will never play with you
again.' Although this threat was serious, we all knew that next
afternoon the three of them would be there again and the
argument of the previous day would be repeated. Grandma
seemed to be amused by these rows, though the shouting
must have upset her, for she had excellent hearing.

I left the house as soon as I could to avoid having to listen
to the shouting of my ancient relatives and went to see my
friend Inge, to discuss with her which poems to choose. She
lived with her mother in a small apartment. I always appreciated the cosy feel and quietness of the place. Inge had two
comfortable armchairs, a small coffee table and a rather small
bed in her room. When we wanted to talk, we usually settled
on the bed, which was covered with a soft woven bedspread.

'Inge,' I said, 'could you help me to choose which poems to read at parents' evening? I'd like to read some of Hviezdoslav's poems. I like his pride in our Slovak nation. I'd also like to read a poem about Štefanik. He really was a hero and helped to liberate us from the Austro-Hungarian oppression.' Inge looked a little doubtful, and with a wistful smile in her large blue eyes she said: 'Are you sure that these poems are the right ones for you to read? They are so nationalistic, and really neither you nor I are truly Slovak.' I felt disappointed with her answer: 'Inge, what are you talking about? Of course we are Slovak. Why would they chose me to read Slovak poetry at parents' evening, if I wasn't Slovak? And anyway, what are we if not Slovak?' Inge smiled and touched my hand: 'Look, it was the Czech teacher who chose you, because you are the best in Slovak classes and write lovely poems yourself. Also the teacher really likes you. But the rest of the class and most of our Slovak friends were outraged, even though they concealed it. Gerti, I really don't know what we are, but look at us – unlike our Slovak schoolmates, we speak German and sometimes Hungarian at home, we go to Jewish religious classes on Sundays and celebrate different holidays from our Slovak countrymen. At home too, our family life is so very different from that of our Slovak friends. Our parents go shopping in Vienna and to the theatre and opera in Budapest. But above all, we are not truly accepted here.'

I sighed, but decided that although I knew that Inge was right, I would read the nationalistic poems I chose. Perhaps I was really yearning to believe that I belonged to Slovakia and was not an outsider in my home.

After this discussion and disagreement we thought that a walk might clear the tension between us. We took our coats and went out in the sunshine to a large park just behind the railway station. It was early spring, and the trees and bushes had started to wake up after the long, cold winter, with tender shoots of green sprouting everywhere. Although spring had arrived and the Easter break was on the doorstep, both of us were still wearing our winter coats and warm, felt boots. We felt comfortably warm and happy gossiping about our friends and planning our Easter holiday. Finally we both headed for home.

By that time it was dusk, and the fading light made the main street of Trnava, paved with grey concrete and flanked with shabby shops, look quite friendly. After Inge left and I was alone I took a shortcut through a tiny narrow street that connected the main street to the marketplace where our house was.

I walked slowly in the dusk and thought about my family. My desire to know where I really belonged was acute.

When I reached our house, I heard soft piano music and I knew my father was back. I ran up the stairs and into the living room, and stopped for a while to watch my father playing. When he saw me he stopped playing and said: 'I hear you have been chosen to read poetry at parents' evening.' Then he took me into his arms. 'Come, Gerti, let us dance together. Should it be a waltz?' I loved dancing with my father. He hummed the tune into my ear, and guided me with great assurance along the parquet floor of our living room. Today it was a Viennese song: *'Wien, nur du allein kannst die Stadt meiner Träume sein'* (Vienna, you alone are the city of my dreams), and we danced together filled with joy. After a while I told him I had to go to my room to work. 'And I have to go out too,' he said, 'but we will all meet when Mother gets home. She will be so proud of you, and will want to hear what poems you are going to read on parents' evening.'

When my mother arrived I charged into her arms. I had missed her so much, and babbled in my haste to tell her all the news. She was pleased, but all she said was: 'Gerti, you really have to give an excellent performance on parents' evening. Do you need help to rehearse? I'll be home next week, perhaps we can discuss how to do the reading best.' She was so very practical, and wonderful.

The 'special day', parents' evening, was held in the assembly hall, and was for parents of the second year. There were about thirty adults present and all the pupils of my year. First there were songs and music, and then the poetry reading followed. Only two pupils read poetry – a boy called Mihálik, and me. When we finished there was great applause and all my classmates congratulated us. The show lasted about one hour, and I felt that this was truly my place, my country and my home. My parents were proud of me and we walked home. No one wanted to spoil my mood; we were very quiet, and my mother put her arm around my shoulders in a protective way.

SUMMER 1939: OUR LIVES CHANGED

My father liked to discuss politics. He had a naive confidence in politicians and believed that they had people's interests at heart. In the years leading up to the war, he meticulously followed the political scene in Western Europe, particularly in France and Great Britain. Once I overheard a conversation between my father and my mother. My father said: 'Jo, it is impossible that England and France will allow Hitler to expand and take over Europe. In fact, it is unthinkable that Hitler would be able to do that. Our Czechoslovakia has incredibly good defences. Built around our borders there is a defence line that no military machinery can cross. The French have their Maginot line, Hitler can not conquer France, and England has the best navy in the world. So it is only a question of time and Hitler will have to give up his expansionist policies.'

My mother, on the other hand, had a healthy scepticism and mistrust of world leaders. 'Look, Max, nobody is going to lift a finger to defend our small Czechoslovakia from Hitler's military power. In spite of all the pacts and assurances, we will soon be occupied. And that will be the end for us Jews here. We have to emigrate, and soon.' But there was nowhere to go. On many occasions I watched my parents, the world map spread in front of them, arguing about where they could go.

7

America and England had a small quota of immigrants whom they would allow to enter the country, but only if someone could guarantee that they would be no burden to the state. My parents had no one in these countries who could vouch for us. But I also sensed the fear my parents felt of leaving the security of the place they knew for an unknown country where they would not be able to speak the language or make a living. Their insecurity and lack of confidence in their ability to survive somewhere else were incomprehensible to me. I gathered from their discussions that there was no room on this planet for us: we just had to stay put and hope for the best.

Although we knew that my father's trust in world politics was misplaced, his infectious optimism was encouraging and helpful not only before, but throughout the difficult times of the war.

When the news came in 1938 that Hitler demanded from Czechoslovakia the *Sudetengebiet* (territories where the majority of the population claimed to be German) and the fascist Hungarian government demanded territories with a predominantly Hungarian population in southern Slovakia, my country was preparing for war to defend itself. My father kept repeating: 'We have the best defence line in Europe, and our people are determined to fight for our wonderful country.' Indeed, Czechoslovakia was a wonderful country, with social services equal to none; it enjoyed prosperity, true freedom and democracy.

Throughout the summer of 1938 the discussions about the fate of my country continued. Chamberlain sent Lord Runciman in July 1938 to observe whether the allegations of the German minority in Czechoslovakia of being discriminated against were justified. Only much later, when I had survived the war and studied this part of my country's history, did I learn that Runciman understood neither the Czech language nor its people, and held discussions only with members of the German upper class. Whatever information he might have gathered and related to Britain must have been inaccurate and biased. Thus Chamberlain was happy to hear what he wanted to believe: that Hitler's demands regarding the *Sudetengebiet* were justified.

And then the fatal meeting between Hitler, British Prime Minister Chamberlain and French Prime Minister Edouard Daladier took place in Munich on 29 September 1938 and a most unfortunate, fatal decision about us was made. Not a single representative from my country was present at the meeting where Hitler's demands were granted. Chamberlain returned home with the vain hope of 'peace in our time'. We were abandoned by everyone.

After Munich all our hopes vanished. We no longer had an invincible defence line, for the borders were changed with no chance left to resist Hitler. Events took their course rather quickly. On 15 March 1939 German troops marched into Bohemia and Moravia and encountered no resistance at all. The Hungarians annexed the border territories of southern Slovakia and a Slovak puppet state was established, with a fascist Catholic priest as head of state with a populist ideology, and no principles. The summer of 1939 was nearly at an end, Europe was on the brink of war and for us all hope had gone.

MARUSHKA

I was just a little over 12 years old on that sunny summer day in 1939, the last day of our school holidays. Now that I was 12, I was allowed to cycle to Uncle Karol's farm in the country, about six miles away from Trnava, alone or with my friends. Today would be perfect for such a trip. Before leaving home I saw Grandma and told her: 'I'd like to visit Uncle Karol today. I hope you don't mind. I'll ask Inge to come with me. Please, Granny, phone Uncle Karol and tell him we'll be there about lunchtime.' 'What a good idea,' Grandma said. 'It's so stuffy and hot in the city, it will be good for you to be out. In any case you sit at home too much, reading books and writing poems. Fresh air will be good for you.'

Encouraged by Grandma I set out to ask Inge to join me. Inge lived quite close to us, on the other side of the square. It was early morning and market day. The square was already full of people. Peasants from the neighbouring villages brought their produce, which included geese that had been force fed to get fat livers for us to eat. There were chickens, piglets, and noisy little kids (baby goats) on offer. The fruit and vegetable section contained melons, peaches, new potatoes and a variety of other products. The peasant women were dressed in their national costumes, with embroidered coloured skirts, blouses, waistcoats and headscarves. The animals and the people bargaining and arguing about the price of the merchandise filled the square with noise. This morning the square was not only lively but also picturesque. Added to this were the smells of fresh onions, vegetables, peaches and melons, mixed with all the animal odours and human sweat. Savouring these impressions, I made my way across the square, avoiding the large horse-drawn carts used by the peasants to bring their wares from the village to the city.

Inge was at home alone, as her mother was working at the local solicitor's office. I hugged her, noticing again how small and delicate-looking she was. She greeted me with a most engaging smile. I asked her whether she could come with me to my uncle's farm. 'Gerti, I'm so sorry, you know how much I like this trip, but I can't leave the flat today, as you see my mother is out working and we are expecting my cousin to visit us any minute. She arrived from Vienna to settle here, is about my age and I promised to look after her.' I was disappointed that Inge couldn't come, but understood her reasons. 'What a pity.' Inge saw that I was disappointed. 'Look, Gerti, you could ask Marushka to go with you. I know she'd like a trip to the country. She always talks about not having enough opportunity to go on trips.' It seemed a good idea, so I went to ask Marushka to come with me. She lived next door to us, and I made my way back across the crowded square.

Marushka and her family lived in a small house, neatly

kept by her mother and painted primrose yellow. She was pleased to be asked and said she would come with me. 'My bicycle is slower than yours – I hope you don't mind that it will slow us down and the journey will take longer.' The trip to my uncle's farm usually took about one hour, so an additional twenty or thirty minutes wouldn't make much difference. We collected our bikes, met outside Marushka's house and were on our way. We planned to have lunch at my uncle's farm and then go fishing in the nearby stream. It was now mid-morning, the heat was getting oppressive, and the smells of animal excrement, hay and human sweat filling the marketplace were becoming quite objectionable. It was time to leave.

We cycled off past the sugar factory, which at this time of the year processed the sugar-beet and emanated the most horrendous stench. In late summer the heat, dust and smells made Trnava an unattractive place. We were delighted to leave it behind us and head for the country, where the gentle breeze blew away the dust and smells of the city. It felt good to be out of the city on such a hot day and to leave behind the noise, the sickly smell of rotting sugar-beet and the dust that was always stirred up on market day by the horses and carts.

The countryside around Trnava is rather flat and dull, but the fertile fields of ripe corn surrounding us were very peaceful. The narrow road we cycled on was unmade, but there was no traffic, and the few horse-drawn carriages did not cause any jams or excessive clouds of dust. After we had cycled for about one hour in the morning heat, we spotted a few trees in a grassy meadow. We were very hot and the shaded spot under the trees seemed an ideal place to rest. We stopped, dismounted from our bicycles and lay down under a tree. The grass was getting dry and prickly, and flies swarmed around us. Nevertheless, lying there in the shade next to each other felt good, and I had a comforting sense of trust and friendship between us.

We were discussing what bait to use for our fishing, and thought we should catch some of the flies that tortured us. I

11

wasn't much good at it, and even when I caught a fly, I couldn't kill it and always let it go. Marushka, on the other hand, was quite an expert: with a swift movement of her hand she caught the flies unaware, then killed them so that we rapidly filled up the box we had prepared for the bait.

I admired Marushka, her skills, her pretty face, corn-coloured hair and confidence. While I was really thin, small and underdeveloped, Marushka, who was only one year older, was already becoming a woman. She had a well-developed figure, and boys eyed her with interest, while I was always treated as a child.

All of a sudden the peaceful silence and sleepy relaxed mood was interrupted by Marushka saying: 'My father said I shouldn't have come out with you today.' I was amazed, for Marushka's father, who worked in our shop as a shop assistant, seemed to like me and was always encouraging our friendship. I remember him getting our horse-drawn carriage ready to take Marushka and me to the swimming pool, which was some distance away from the town and belonged to the sugar factory. He was always kind and very nice to me. 'Why not?' I asked. Marushka blushed. 'He said that because you are Jews, you will soon be taken away, and then he will be able to take over your father's shop and we will move into your house. But we must show that we do not like mixing with Jews and that we approve of the National Socialist principles. My father joined the Hlinka party a month ago, so he knows about these things.'

I kept silent, but the pleasure and enjoyment of having an outing with a friend were gone. After a while I asked Marushka: 'And what do you think about this? We've always been good friends, could you just forget it?' Marushka avoided my eyes, and looked somewhere beyond me. Finally she said:' I don't know what to think, I'm confused and will miss you, but if it's going to make it difficult for my family that I have a Jewish friend, I'll have to stop seeing you.' 'That isn't really what I meant,' I replied. 'I want to know what you think about the plans that Jews should be sent away and you and others should just take over their property. Anyway, have you thought about where we might be sent to?' Marushka was clearly embarrassed, but nevertheless said: 'Everyone says that you had too much money, that you exploited us and that it's time for the people to take over everything. Well, you are richer than my family, aren't you? They will send you to a work camp, and everyone thinks that it will be good for you to learn to work hard, while the people you have exploited enjoy themselves. I think that this is just, and although I'll miss you, it will be nice to live in your house.' I was stunned by Marushka's total lack of compassion, feeling of justice and crude greed. Marushka continued to list the advantages and material gains she would have when we were sent away. Life for her would be so much better – why care about us?

I no longer wanted to go anywhere with Marushka. I felt I just wanted to be at home with my family. I told Marushka that she may as well stop seeing her Jewish friend now, and that I would like to return home. I picked up my bicycle and was getting ready to be on my way. To my surprise Marushka tried to stop me, arguing: 'But today we could have enjoyed ourselves.' I was deeply hurt and felt let down and shocked by her callousness. Even though she no longer wanted to be a friend and was enthusiastic about us being dispatched to some unknown destination while she and her family took over our house, she was still prepared to take advantage of me today. So I didn't say anything, and silently cycled home far ahead of Marushka. I felt that I never wanted to see her again.

I arrived home and the familiar, cosy atmosphere of our house eased the hurt. My father and my grandmother were at home. They were sitting in the small bright room furnished with cane furniture that I liked so very much. They asked me what was wrong. I didn't want to worry them, so I just said that I wasn't feeling well and went up to my room. I sat down by the desk, where I had my books, and a special small notebook which was my diary. I opened it and described the events of this morning, and then concluded: 'This morning is the end not only of my summer holiday but also of many other good things and dreams of my happy carefree childhood. It is probably the end of my childhood.'

AUTUMN 1939: EXCLUDED FROM SCHOOL

Next day school started. Our gymnasium was a co-educational school with very mixed intake. There were several children from the neighbouring villages and some Czech students, and our teachers were a mixture of Czech and Slovak nationalities.

The morning when school started was warm and pleasant. The first lesson was religious instruction for Catholic pupils, and non-Catholic children did not have to attend. So we went to school one hour later than the Catholic children. When I arrived at the school gate, there were already several other children, some Jewish, some Czech, standing outside the closed gate. On the gate hung a big notice saying: 'Jews and Czechs are excluded from school.' There were about a dozen of us; children ranging from 11 to 18 years of age. We stood there not knowing what to do, speechless and desperately disappointed to be excluded. We wanted to talk to someone, to have some explanation as to what was going on. We wanted to know what our friends thought of this. So we rang the bell and hammered at the gate. No one came to talk to us. I was particularly friendly with one boy, Mihalik, who wrote beautiful poetry and later in Communist Czechoslovakia became quite a well-known poet. I shouted his name, and others asked to speak to their best friends. All we got in reply from the children was a chorus of shouts: 'Jews out, Czechs out.' They also shouted some obscenities and no one stopped them. Not a single child or teacher came out to talk to us. Some of the older children among us had been attending the school for many years and had many friends and teachers that knew them well, yet not one of them came out to talk to us. Those of us standing outside the gate felt betrayed and confused.

We didn't know whether to wait or to go home. We couldn't understand, let alone believe, what was happening. Finally, after about one hour, we became angry. But we were not given a chance to argue our case. Nobody would talk to us, and we knew that if we waited for the school day to finish and for the children to leave school they would probably not only not talk to us, but might beat us up to show off in front of the others.

Suddenly, as our anger mounted, we felt that we just couldn't leave without some action and passively accept this humiliation. A plan suddenly occurred to me. Many of the children cycled to school and their bicycles were in the back yard. If we could damage their bicycles, it would at least make them remember this day as an unpleasant time, which we very much wanted. After a brief discussion we decided to carry out this plan, and inflict some damage on the bicycles. We had to be careful, because we wanted all the problems to appear the result of accidents that had happened on the way to school. So we loosened screws, damaged the valves of the tyres, and put sharp small stones between wheel rims and tyres. Then we went home disgusted with everything, including ourselves for ruining the bicycles. There was not much satisfaction in knowing that not one of the cyclists would arrive home safely, but it was something, it was a gesture to show that we would not accept without resistance what they did to us.

Back at home I told my parents what had happened at school. Strangely, they did not seem to be surprised. My mother, with her usual ability to see the practical consequences of events, decided that I should do a secretarial course which was private and run by a pleasant elderly gentleman. I should learn typing, shorthand and other secretarial skills. This course was held only two evenings a week, however, and I needed to be occupied during the rest of the time.

There were many new courses where various crafts were being taught and my mother asked me what I wanted to learn. I told her: 'Mother, you know how clumsy I am, I'll be lousy at any handicraft. But Inge is doing a course, and I'd like to go with her. At least we will be together.' So we went together to learn how to make artificial flowers. Unfortunately for me, I was really clumsy, and only managed because Inge helped to finish my attempts to make something that looked vaguely like a flower.

Occasionally I did see my old school friends, but they never acknowledged me. Most evenings young people walked along the high street. These 'promenades' served as a meeting place for girls and boys, where they flirted, giggled and explored their social skills. The girls would be all dressed up, and the boys would show off, laughing and joking. It was a centre of social life, where girls and boys in their teens flirted with each other, and if lucky moved into the darker recesses of a nearby park for other activities. A few weeks after being excluded from school I saw Marushka with a much older young man leaving the high street and heading towards the park. She did not show any sign of recognizing me. I felt disappointed and deceived. It also seemed to me that I was missing out on something that other people of my age experienced and enjoyed.

POLITICAL EDUCATION

Being excluded from mixing and interacting with my former friends made me look for other company. I joined a group of young Jews who, like me, were excluded from school and had to take their education into their own hands. Like me, they were thirsty for knowledge, and not being allowed a formal education hurt. I could identify with them and felt that we belonged together. Many of us Jewish teenagers started to meet regularly outside the town, on a large meadow called 'the pond', because years ago it had been a pond. Now this large quiet meadow was a good meeting place for us. There were about twenty of us – Inge, me, my cousin Klári, her boyfriend Ernest, the son of my primary schoolteacher Jan, my

16

future husband Walter (Rudi), and several others. We had heady discussions as to how best organize the world. The bitter feeling of being excluded gradually subsided. Apart from Jan, Klári, Walter, Inge and me, none of us survived the war.

I was attracted to Walter. He was two years older than I was, and I considered him handsome. He had a round, friendly face and a winning smile. I thought most of the people were cleverer than I was, but Walter was truly exceptional. Gradually I began to like him more then any of the others.

A topic hotly discussed by us all was Zionism. We knew that there were secret organizations that were arranging illegal emigration to Palestine, where Jews fought and worked towards building up and acquiring their own country. One of my cousins emigrated in this way to Palestine and survived the war, but he was a bit older and perhaps less involved in theoretical questions of the rights and wrongs of Zionism. The Zionist spirit, which included a pride in being Jewish, was important for us at the time for it helped to maintain our self-esteem when faced with constant humiliations at the hands of our Slovak neighbours. Nevertheless, we fastidiously considered the rights and wrongs of this ideology. We were deeply influenced by socialist principles and read Marx, Lenin and Trotsky. From the socialist point of view Zionism was yet another nationalist movement that, in the long run, would not solve the ailments of the world we lived in. I remember feeling helpless and inadequate, for my understanding of these problems was so poor that I could not subscribe to any solution discussed, be it Zionism, communism or democracy.

1940–42: OUR FIGHT FOR DIGNITY

Time passed and gradually, almost without our noticing it, our lives changed beyond recognition. To enforce the rules of the fascist state a special 'police' had been formed – the so-called Hlinka Guard. They emulated the German SS and

Gestapo, wore black uniforms and walked about in black boots. Their main purpose was to harass Jews and those Slovaks who tried to be decent. Soon we Jews were ordered to wear a yellow Star of David all the time. We were not allowed to go to cinemas and we were forbidden to go to the skating rink. There was a curfew, and we had to be in by 9 o'clock. All Jewish shops or other enterprises had to have an Aryan to supervise them and above all to steal the profits. In our shop it was Marushka's father who took this role, and he was not kind at all. He quite shamelessly stole from us what he could. But even worse than these humiliations were the beatings of old, helpless Jews that had become regular events in our town, and were usually carried out by people who not so long ago had appeared to be friendly.

KATE'S STORY

One day as I walked along the narrow lane that connected the main street with the cobbled square where our house stood, I heard screams coming from one of the doorways. I went to see what was happening and saw two uniformed men, one of whom was Marushka's brother, beating my old Auntie Kate. Her white hair was loose and the men pulled it to prevent her protecting her face. She was sprawled out on the pavement as the men kicked her and laughed. In my anger I didn't think very clearly what I was doing, for what I did wasn't very sensible. The men were so involved in the beating, they hadn't noticed my approach, so I rapidly leaped towards the group, grabbed Auntie Kate round her shoulders, pulled her up and ran, dragging her behind me. The assailants were so surprised that it took them a while to decide what to do. This gave us time to reach our house, which was just around the corner. I quickly got into the house dragging Aunt Kate behind me and locked the door. My grandmother was immediately on the scene, helping to calm Auntie Kate and attending to her bruises. Poor Grandma, she couldn't help telling Auntie Kate off, as though it was her fault she had been beaten: 'Why on earth did you take the short cut through the narrow lane, which is notorious for such attacks?' Although deaf, Auntie Kate must have guessed what Grandma had said for she proudly retorted: 'Well, we ought not to be prevented from using the streets of our city.' I admired her, for in spite of her ordeal Auntie Kate was indignant and self-righteous, adding: 'I am not going to be intimidated by these hooligans.'

I then went to the shop and found our former shop assistant, now the new owner of the shop, whose son had been involved in the beating. Being young and naive I tried to talk to him, and was astonished that he didn't show a trace of shame – on the contrary, it seemed to me that he quite approved of his son attacking a helpless old woman. Finally he told me: 'It will not be long now, and all of you will be gone.'

DEALING WITH HUMILIATION

It was astonishing for us young people how the adults accepted the situation. They believed it was temporary, and that it would all be over soon and they would be able to continue living amidst those who had betrayed and humiliated them as though nothing had happened. Yet not all of our Slovak friends deserted us: some remained loyal.

One day when I was hovering about in our house, my father's friend Mr Pavelka came to visit. He was a farmer in his late forties with a cheerful face and kind eyes that reflected his personality. On that day, he lowered his big frame into the cane chair which creaked under his weight, and said to my father: 'If you want us to keep any of your possessions for you, my wife and I have decided that we will hide them and when all this is over we will return them to you. In case you have to leave suddenly, or if the Slovak Hlinka Guard wants to confiscate Jewish property, at least they will not find much.' Pavelka was right and he was a true and honest friend, so my mother wrapped up our silver, her jewellery and a few things she cherished and handed them to Pavelka in a large brown parcel. When he left I asked my mother: 'Do you really believe we will need these things when all this is over?' My mother was taken aback by my question and said: 'When all this is over and if we survive, we will need something to start up again. This may just help us to do so. It also may be helpful to have something we can trade in during the next difficult years.' How very right she was! But at the time I couldn't imagine that this very Pavelka and maybe our jewellery would save my life a few years later.

For us young people it was much harder to accept the humiliations. The aggressive Zionist ideology that we teenagers often discussed during our evening meetings in the meadow helped us to plan and carry out several gestures of defiance without which children of our age would have felt even more frustrated. So, for example, when we were no longer allowed into the skating rink we made up our minds to see what would happen if we tried to enter it. The rink usually opened at 5 o'clock in the afternoon. One afternoon we peacefully approached the entrance, bought tickets and asked to be admitted. The ticket collector who stood at the small wooden gate looked at us in amazement, noticed our yellow Stars of David and said: 'But you are not permitted to enter, you are Jews.' The oldest and most diplomatic person in our group was Jan, and he said: 'But our friends here told us that they will make sure that we are allowed in.' By this time many of the 'friends' were already by the gate shouting at us, 'Jews out, we don't want you here.' Most of our former 'friends' were now completely enmeshed in Fascism and belonged to the Hlinka Youth, an organization similar to the Hitler Youth. They showed no sympathy for us, mocked us and laughed at us. Disappointed, but perhaps not too surprised, we decided on some form of retaliation. We knew exactly where our Slovak friends would split up after leaving the skating rink to go to their homes. Although there was a curfew for us Jews and we were not allowed to stay out after dark we decided to defy it, and took off our yellow Stars of David. We planned to ambush three of the most violent fascist youths, two boys and one girl, on their way home. We smeared our faces with soot and used all sorts of camouflage, then waited for our victims. We did succeed in ambushing those three and beating them up, but none of us really got any satisfaction out of this and we were in fact embarrassed about our behaviour. Yet in a strange way it helped us to feel better. It made us feel that we were not just lying down and accepting all the humiliation, but were trying to preserve our dignity. Throughout these few last years at home our theoretical evening discussions continued, but our endeavours to find a recipe to create a better world were not altogether successful.

Perhaps because of these traumatic events and drastic changes in our lives, strong and quite mature bonds, friendships and love were forged during this time among many of us. My cousin Klári, 15 years old, was deeply in love with Ernest. They used to walk together holding hands and kissing. In some way the knowledge that all could end so soon, as indeed it did, gave these young relationships a special intensity. I was very much in love with Walter. At the time, however, I was seriously let down. He was nice and friendly, but that was all. When we arranged to meet on our own so we could be alone for a while he never turned up. He later told me that this was on account of my childish hat with a pom-pom, which made me look like a 9-year-old girl, and that he was too embarrassed to go around with a child. So I felt really rejected, and in some way this feeling that I was not attractive to men stayed with me. It is strange that, faced with all the really serious problems we had, we could nevertheless be affected by the same emotions as normal teenagers.

As the situation for us Jews relentlessly worsened our evening discussions were getting much more concerned with our immediate future. One evening Ernest asked: 'Where do you think we will be sent?' Jan, the oldest of the group, was optimistic: 'Into work camps,' he said. 'We will probably have to work very hard, and will get very little food.' This made a terrible impression on me, and I was consumed with trying to work out how one could somehow re-use one's body and survive without food. It was with this in mind that I started to bite my nails and chew them, so as not to waste any parts of my body. I did not try to recycle any other discarded parts, though.

Our parents were also helpless and had no idea what to do. My father was hoping that the war would end before anything serious happened. He could not believe that all the might of France and England could not halt the German progress. Not even all Hitler's victories and his capture of most of Europe eroded my father's hope. The months and years went by and we were growing up in a hostile environment with adults close to us unable to change the situation.

All the meetings, discussions and reading of books could not replace the social environment of a school. In addition, our first experience of the adult world was that of hostility, threats and injustice. It was an extraordinary two years of growing up, yet it didn't prepare us for what really did happen in 1942 and later.

SPRING 1942: THE SHATTERED GLASS

Like most years, members of our close family gathered at my grandmother's house for Passover. My numerous uncles, aunts and cousins all came to spend this festival that celebrated freedom from bondage together at my grandmothers house which she shared with my parents. I slept on the sofa in the sitting room because my aunt who was visiting from Budapest slept in my bedroom. Unlike my bedroom window the window of the sitting room faced the square and one night the rioting crowds targeted it. The next morning I woke up to see the remnants of the window on my bed and in the room. The shattered glass glissened as the brilliant clear April sunrays hit it. Carefully, I got out of bed and stood amidst the broken glass on my favourite carpet, the red silky

22

Persian one, that gave the room its warm glow. I couldn't understand how one broken window pane could have provided so much glass. I realized that the window must have been broken by a stone thrown by the crowds during last night's riots. I heard the noise and shouting, but then fell asleep and miraculously managed to sleep, shutting the noise of the crowds out of my mind. Thus, I neither noticed nor heard the stone and the noise made by the shattered window. Now fully awake I tried awkwardly to avoid the pieces of broken glass, as I moved towards the other window to look at the street. Outside the cobbled square, the town's market place was deserted. People were sleeping in after last night's riots, when ours and other Jewish homes and shops had been smashed and looted. I left the window, dressed and cleaned up the room. Now fully awake it was time to turn my attention to the present. I checked the room again for small shreds of glass, and when I was satisfied I left the room and went into the kitchen.

My grandmother was busy preparing breakfast, put a cup filled with broken matzo in front of me and a jug of coffee. 'Grandma, how come that in spite of everything you manage to look after us all and remember what we like to eat and drink?' Grandma smiled and said: 'Well, maybe being well looked after and calm will help us to consider our future and make the right decisions.'

After breakfast, my parents, grandmother, aunts and uncles from Budapest gathered in the sitting room and discussed what to do when it became necessary to leave home. The only option seemed to be to cross the border between Slovakia and Hungary illegally and somehow live in Hungary. My father said with great anguish and a clarity quite unusual for him: 'But if we have to leave home and escape to Hungary, what will we do there? We will have no money and we will not be able to work. I know we can get forged papers, but it would be too risky to get a job. I can't imagine how we will live.'

Uncle Arthur, my mother's brother, a large man with a bald

head, thick glasses and self-assured gestures, replied: 'I know how you feel, but this is an emergency and when your lives are at stake there is no way we can be proud. As you know we are quite rich, and what better way to spend our money then to help each other. I can support you for as long as it takes, provided nothing terrible happens in Hungary, but then all of us will be in the same boat.' I saw my mother looking with great affection at her older brother. They had a special relationship: my mother being 20 years younger, Arthur always felt protective towards her and she admired him, and rightly so. He had left his native village when he was 16, and had gone to Budapest without a penny. Within the next ten years he had managed to build up a prosperous textile factory and had become very wealthy. He had also married my father's younger sister, Ada, and so our families were doubly related. My aunts and uncles, who lived in Hungary, assured us that they would look after us there and that they would get things ready for us in case we had to flee. All this was comforting but, in spite of all the signs to the contrary, I was not ready to accept the reality that we might have to escape and leave home. Against all odds I still had hopes that it would not come to that.

FIRST DEPORTATIONS

Just a few days later, in April 1942, those of us who were over 16 had to report for deportation. Only very few of our group that met regularly in our meadow were not yet 16, and most of them were deported then. A few of us went into hiding, or, like my cousins Klári and Margaret, escaped across the border to Hungary, where with the help of the family they somehow managed to live. Walter also tried to escape to Hungary but had no one there to help him and was caught by the Hungarian militia, beaten up and thrown back across the border to Slovakia. He was then sent with others to a concentration camp in Poland.

PREPARING TO LEAVE HOME

A few days after the young Jews over 16 were deported, there was a family gathering in our living room and I overheard a conversation that worried me. Uncle Hans was pure Aryan and German. He was married to my father's sister Olga, and always helped our family. One evening he returned from a pub where he had had a drink with the local chief constable and described the conversation he had had with him. The constable had tried to be sympathetic and had told him that he was aware of the fact that Hans's wife Olga was Jewish and that her family had lived in Trnava for a long time and its members were law-abiding good citizens. He then told Hans that as a friend of the family he had to warn him that within the next few months most of the Slovak Jews would have to be resettled and leave their homes. This was a government order. He mentioned that it had already been made clear to the Jews that they were unwanted. They were no longer allowed to go to public places and schools. Their valuables had been confiscated; Aryans had been put into their businesses to supervise the Jewish owners and cream off most of the earnings. So it had been made clear that they were not wanted here, yet many of them had not taken the hint and had not left their homes. He thought that Hans's wife and her family seemed to believe that they belonged here, but this was not so. He then asked Hans to warn us all and tell us that since we were Jews nothing could save us from deportation.

Hans, who although not a Jew belonged to our family, shook his head in sorrow. His grey, calm eyes looked troubled as he said to my father: 'You know, Max, myself being a German makes all this more difficult. I feel deeply ashamed for my German countrymen and for being a German, and yet there is nothing I can do about it, just like you and Olga can do nothing about being Jewish.' Then after a while he added: 'But perhaps we can each of us do just a tiny bit to make it harder for the fascists to carry out their plans. Neither of us is a hero, but to allow our own neighbours and friends to be

25

dragged away to an unknown destination, where there is no guarantee that they will be resettled, is too much to accept. Could we let as many families as possible know what is planned for them?'

'We can try,' my father Max replied, 'but will they believe us? Look, we had the cattle trucks filled with Austrian Jews passing through our town, the people inside were screaming, they were hungry, thirsty and crowded and we all heard their screams, yet none of us believes even now that this will happen to us.'

After a while Hans said quietly: 'Can you blame us that we have more trust in human dignity than is justified?' Finally Hans said that we would have to make some arrangements in order to avoid being sent away in the dreaded cattle trucks to an unknown destination. There was silence in the room; no one wanted to believe this message, yet we all knew he was right. My Uncle Karol had a son, Martin, who was mentally deficient and Karol's first thought was to find a place to hide him. 'But who would hide him?' he asked. I was astonished. Karol, with his large estate, many employees and friends among the local people, could not find someone to hide Martin?

Then my grandma spoke to her two daughters from Budapest: 'Manci and Ada, you go back home to Budapest immediately while the rest of us prepare an escape route to Budapest for those who need it. It looks as though in Hungary things are not yet so bad for the Jews, and Admiral Horthy may not give way to the German pressure to have the Hungarian Jews deported. But I will not go anywhere. At 75 it is too hard to escape, and I may be able to help here and organize things.'

Strangely, even at this time there was talk about property, possessions, and material provision for the future. This I could not understand, and I found it silly. I was exhausted and fell asleep, then suddenly I was woken up by the sound of a train passing through. I thought I heard screams and sighs and that those locked in the cattle trucks were my parents and family.

2 *Leaving Home*

Soon after this last family meeting, one evening, when I was trying to occupy myself by learning how to type, our doorbell rang and I went to open the door. My father's friend Mr Pavelka was at the door. When I opened the door to let him in his nice warm brown eyes smiled at me and I thought that he could be trusted. Now, when he entered our house he seemed restless and agitated. 'Please tell your father that I need to talk to him. It's urgent.' My father was asleep, and I suggested to Mr Pavelka that perhaps their conversation could wait till tomorrow. 'No,' Mr Pavelka said with unexpected firmness, 'Go and wake him up.' It was more an order then a request and I didn't argue any more, for I was certain that Mr Pavelka had something very serious to tell my father, something that could change our lives. My father must have heard us talking, for he suddenly appeared at the door wide awake.

Pavelka and my father shook hands, went into the living room and left me outside. I settled in the cosy hall with the white wicker chairs and sat down waiting for the outcome of the conversation, guessing at the news Pavelka had brought us. I had a foreboding that he had come to tell us that we would have to leave.

Sitting there expecting soon to be told to leave home, I tried to observe and commit to memory all the objects around me: the pictures, the little table and my favourite porcelain figurine of a shepherd with a flute. Somehow I knew that these were the last few hours that I would spend in the house that was my home, and that the familiar objects of my happy childhood would soon be but faint memories quite unimportant in face of things to come. My eyes were watering, although I tried to keep a hold of myself and did not allow myself to cry. And yet, in spite of my effort to remember my childhood, and all that mattered to me then, later on when I survived I remembered little of my home.

My father came out, interrupting my sentimental self-pitying mood. His shoulders were slumped, his hazel eyes were sad, and the smile was gone from his face. I knew then for certain that the news was bad. I put my arms around his shoulders and tried to comfort him. He looked pale, sad and somehow defeated. I understood that his grief was due to the realization that he could not protect us from what was to come. Very quietly he said: 'We have to leave the house tonight. My friend has just told me that he has heard from very reliable sources that tomorrow morning the local government is preparing to round up all the Jews in Trnava who do not have a special permit to stay, to be deported the same day. No one seems to know where the Jews are being sent to, but it is better not to be included in the transport. To avoid it we have to leave immediately. I am going to discuss what to do with the rest of the family. You try to get ready.' Although I had expected this, the fact that it was now for real made my feelings about leaving home and my anxiety about the future truly painful.

Where could we go? It could only be Hungary, but how could we get there and what would happen to my grandma? I remembered that some preparations as to what to do if faced with an emergency like this had been discussed. My Uncle Hans had worked out some plan to get us to Hungary, where my favourite Aunt Manci lived and where Admiral Horthy still managed to keep his Jews safe. But there were still many questions in my mind that scared me. Would we have to hide in some obscure, dark hiding place, without being able to go out and breathe in fresh air? I could not bear the thought of such an existence, and instinctively knew that I could not survive it.

My mother moved about the flat making all the arrangements for our departure. She was putting some things into
suitcases that were later to be taken to us in Hungary by Hans
and packing a few things into small carrier bags that we
would take with us. She wore a casual outfit, trousers and a
loose jumper. She was in complete control of herself, and it
seemed of the situation as well. She was calm and her voice
quiet, without any sign of panic. 'How can she be so cool?' I
thought, but kept quiet. 'Gerti, go and pack a few things, but
very few, only as much as you can comfortably carry during a
long strenuous walk. Don't take anything you will not need
immediately. We are leaving straight away. The plan is as
follows: you and I are going to stay with our friend Jane [my
piano teacher] overnight and during the daytime tomorrow.
Then in the evening we will try to cross the border to
Hungary. Father says he will follow us later. He has decided to
go separately, because he thinks two women are less conspicuous during an illegal border crossing.' Even though he might
be right, I resented being separated from him and would have
liked him to come with us tonight, but Uncle Hans, who had
made the arrangements, persuaded me that Father's plan was
better. Grandma, I was told, would stay home for the time
being. There was no danger for her yet. To fool us, we were
told that only Jews young enough to work would be deported
to work camps and that my grandma was too old. How very
naive we all were!

There was no time to say goodbye to friends, and maybe it
was better that way. It would have been too painful, and I
knew that if I was to survive I had to find ways to protect
myself from pain and many other ordinary normal feelings a
young girl of my age usually experiences. Such feelings were
dangerous and were luxuries I could not afford. I felt in every
fibre of my body that the fight for survival had started in
earnest, and I was determined to do my best to win. I knew I
needed much luck and a lot more, but I was just 15 and life
seemed so full of promise, a gift that I was determined to fight
for and keep.

I tried to choose the right things to wear for our border crossing. Perhaps one needed to wear things as for a school trip, I thought. So I chose some outfits that fitted this type of activity. I also packed a toothbrush, a comb and other bits and pieces in a small bag my mother gave me. Equipped with this luggage I went to Jane's flat; my mother was to follow later. Jane lived in an old house just one storey high where the flats were built around a square courtyard. I always imagined that this was typical of Spanish houses, but there were a few houses like this in Trnava. Jane's flat was one of those where the door and the windows faced the courtyard, so no one from the street could peep in.

Jane was a slim woman in her early 50s. She was a music teacher who lived alone and had no children. My memories of her were clouded by her attempts to teach me to play the piano. I hated these lessons, and at the age of 6 to 7, when my parents made me go to her, I always ended up crying rather than playing the piano. She was devoted to music, and could not understand how anyone could dislike learning to play the piano. She was a good friend of my mother, and both my mother and Jane tried to help to persuade me to love playing music. Now, back in her flat, I felt guilty for having been so difficult. She certainly was a real friend and took a great risk by hiding us for a day and night in her small cramped lodgings.

For me, cooped up in the flat and waiting there was almost unbearable. I was unable to read, knit, or do anything during this time, and paced restlessly from one end of the tiny room to the other, until it irritated my mother and I was told to stop. Although we waited barely twenty-four hours, it seemed to me an eternity. Looking back, this waiting required more control and effort than all my other, much more strenuous, later activities. My mother coped much better. To me she seemed completely unperturbed, quietly knitting a jumper for me she had started a while ago. How could she do it? It was quite likely that I would never wear it. Would I be around and alive in one month's time, I wondered. Jane looked after us and provided us with food, which I couldn't swallow. She played the piano for us, and tried to engage me in conversation, but I was unable to respond to her kindness, and just waited for the time to pass. I didn't know time could pass that slowly.

After a restless night and endless day, dusk gradually appeared. At last the waiting was over, and it was time for my mother and me to leave and meet the taxi, as arranged by Hans. My mother and I took our small bags and left. We passed the empty street and the Franciscan church at the end of the street that we were hiding in. I noticed the hill to my right which, in the winter, I used to charge down on my sledge. All that was so very far away, as though it had never happened. Now, in our drab clothes that were suitable for walking in the country, dark colours that would blend into the night, but also pass as unobtrusive in a village, we were almost invisible, and this was somehow symbolic, for we were indeed losing our identity. All this blended well with my mood of accepting a final irrevocable change in my life.

The place we were to meet the taxi was in a part of Trnava I didn't know at all. Most of the houses were dilapidated, and the streets were not paved. I was cold and frightened. By the time the taxi arrived it was completely dark. My mother and I had scarves tied around our heads, like countrywomen. We were lucky, for our appearance was such that both of us could pass easily for local peasants. My mother was fair with blue eyes, small, and had strong arms and legs, which gave her an appearance of someone used to physical work. I had corn-coloured hair, grey eyes, a straight nose and a happy face. I was plump and vivacious, and the fear we felt did not show on either of us. In short, we did not look Jewish. Even then, I felt ashamed for being pleased about it.

The taxi was waiting for us at the arranged place, and my Uncle Hans was there too. Hans gave my mother some Hungarian money and told us about the arrangements that had been made: the taxi would take us to the border, where we would be met by a guide who would cross the

Slovak–Hungarian border with us. After this briefing we said goodbye to Uncle Hans and were left alone in the street. The taxi driver was a cheerful middle-aged man. He motioned to us and we entered the battered black car. I couldn't help being frightened. How reliable was this man? Would he take us to the border or to the Slovak fascist authorities? These thoughts raced through my head as I sat in the taxi, clinging to my mother, who seemed much more confident. Then I gradually calmed down.

We sat quietly in the taxi as the driver headed south towards the border. On our way we passed the flat country-side with the rich farmland that I knew so well. Through the open window of the car we could smell the familiar scent of manure, spread onto the fields at this time of the year. Fortunately there was no moon, it was a very dark night and this meant that it was a favourable night for crossing the border. But during the ride in the taxi it was hard for us not to think about the sad fact that this trip marked the end of our life in our home, and what would follow would be a difficult struggle for survival.

Yet I couldn't help feeling exhilarated; after all, this escape in the middle of the night was a real, true adventure and it had to be successful. Mixed with the exhilaration there was a premonition of things to come, a fear of the yet unknown forces that were being summoned to destroy the life of my family and my people. For the first time I was determined to outwit the 'enemy', and survive at almost any cost. I don't know whether this intense desire to live at almost any cost is the privilege of the very young or was part of me. At the time I believed it to be a normal reaction for a young person, but my later experience and observations of other young people make me believe it was rather typical of me. So great was my confidence on that night that I believed there must be bound-less possibilities for anyone with courage and imagination to outwit those who threatened our lives. The millions of victims who perished in Hitler's concentration camps bear witness to a different reality. My thoughts were interrupted when the car stopped and we seemed to have arrived at our destination, the edge of a small village near the border with Hungary.

We got out of the taxi and my mother paid the driver. Again, I was wondering whether, now that the taxi driver had his money, he would betray us. Unlike my mother I was much less inclined to trust the people who helped us, and doubt always lingered at the back of my mind.

Outside, the air was chilly and it was pitch dark. Somehow, out of nowhere, a tall young man materialized and told us that he was our guide. He said he would now look after us and he took control of the situation. Unlike the taxi driver, somehow his personality inspired complete confidence, and I felt no fear at all, either of betrayal or of his ability to get us across the border safely. Any worry that our crossing of the border might fail was completely dispelled by the competent and professional attitude of this young man. I saw him only on that single occasion, and have no idea what became of him, but I will never forget him.

He said that we would have to walk through the village very quietly, mainly because we had to avoid alerting the dogs. If they started barking, the border patrol might hear them and we certainly did not want to alert them. We knew of course that being discovered by the police, or rather the border guards, would be the end of our escape, but the presence of our guide made this option seem impossible. In the darkness the three of us crept quietly along the unmade dirt track that was the main road through the village. The village was quiet and by its very peacefulness it gave the impression of being full of unexpected danger. We were relieved when we emerged at the southern end of the village. The young man led us through a small wood, and just before reaching the clearing, he told us to lie down so that we would be protected from being seen by trees and bushes. There, at the edge of the wood, we waited for what seemed a very long time. Then we heard footsteps and saw the border patrol in their green uniforms making their round. As soon as the soldiers passed the clearing, our young guide signalled to us to follow him. Now we walked swiftly across a meadow and a field, both of which seemed dangerously exposed, but the dark, moonless night protected us. After about one hour's walk across the fields the young man pointed to a few houses ahead of us and explained that this was Diószeg, a village on the Hungarian side of the border, and that we were now in Hungary. He said he would have to leave us now so that he could get back before dawn. He advised us to wait here until the morning, for it was safer to enter Diószeg in daytime. With this final warning the young man disappeared so quickly that there wasn't even time to thank him. Yet both of us felt deep gratitude for our guide, who had made us feel so safe in his charge.

Dawn came fast, and with it the start of a new day. Different sounds filled the air; the cockerel and his hens led the chorus of noises, and among them human voices speaking Hungarian reached me. I could not understand or speak a single word of Hungarian. The excitement and exhilaration I felt during the night vanished, and gave way to fear. I was worried that if I was approached by anyone, I could never pass as a Hungarian peasant girl without being able to speak Hungarian, and would be taken for what I was: a refugee from Slovakia. My mother seemed to have guessed what was on my mind, and said: 'Don't worry, I will do all the talking. It will not seem strange, since to most people you look too young and inexperienced to make any decisions.' With her extraordinary sense for practicalities and feeling what needed to be done, my mother reached for her blue address book and took it out of her bag. 'We have to reach Maryshka Néni's house. She lives in Diószeg, and hopefully can help us to board the train for Budapest and give us some more Hungarian money. But we must reach her house unobserved, so as not to endanger her. I am trying to find her address.' As my mother was leafing through her address book she said: 'We can not hang about on the street this time of the day, for the police or border guards will be suspicious. We have to get to Maryshka's house quickly, get a few hours rest, and clean up after the border crossing.' I was worried about going to the railway station and boarding the train, for stations near the border were heavily policed and very often it was there that refugees were caught and that was what we now were: refugees.

The church bells rang for morning mass and I suddenly noticed two uniformed figures, wearing tall peaked hats with bright feathers on them. These were the most feared Hungarian border guards, renowned for their brutality and sadism. I grabbed my mother's arm and walked towards the place where the sound of the church bells originated, hoping that an attendance of the morning mass in a church would be a suitable place to hide. There was a church only a few steps in front of us, and both of us quickly entered it. We were almost certain that we were not spotted by the guards. Once in the church, however, neither of us knew what to do and how to behave in order to look as though we belonged there. My mother had never been in a Catholic church, but I had occasionally accompanied my friends to the church, and quite liked the organ music and the lavishly decorated inside of Catholic churches. Now I tried to recall what they did in there. 'There is this container with water', I recalled, 'and you dip your fingers into it, then you touch your forehead, stomach, left and finally right shoulder. This makes the sign of the cross.' I rapidly instructed my mother what to do, and we went through the drill. Then we walked towards the centre of the church where several women were kneeling absorbed in prayer, and we did the same.

After a while, when we thought that the streets would be busier we walked towards the exit of the church and my mother asked a woman we saw just outside the church to direct us towards the street where my aunt Maryshka had her house.

We got there safely. I was delighted to discover that my uncle Hans was already there, preparing everything we might need to board the train. He was much relieved to see us, and told us with a grin on his face that he had had every faith in us getting there. He seemed in a wonderful mood, chatting to me about my adventure and teasing me that I had fallen for my guide. His good mood was infectious, and we soon relaxed. Then everyone was keen to send us off for a bath and rest. Maryshka's house was large, with many bedrooms but only one bathroom, where the water was heated in a large cylinder by a wooden fire. The enamelled bath was large and comfortable and we enjoyed it, but it did not wash away our fears. Then we went to bed, but I was too excited to be able to sleep. Finally, the tiredness and the comfort and relief that we had got there safely helped me to fall asleep. After what seemed a very short time, we were woken up and told to prepare for the journey. Maryshka fed us a wonderful meal and packed a hamper with food for our journey to Budapest. We said our goodbyes to her and were ready to go . Then Hans put his arm round my shoulder, took my mother by the hand and we were on our way to the station. With Hans with us I felt safe. He waited with us until the old steam train arrived, puffing big clouds of steam. Then he chose a carriage for us, helped us to board the train and stood on the platform waving to us until the train departed. He would have accompanied us, he said, but he wanted to wait for the arrival of my father in the next few days. I wished my father were with us.

In spite of our rest in Maryshka's house we were very tired. The emotional upset of leaving home, the border crossing and finding our way undiscovered to my aunt's house left us exhausted. The uncertain future and worry about the safety of my father contributed to our gloom. In spite of all that, when we finally slumped onto the wooden seats, I fell into a deep sleep, and woke up only on arrival in Budapest.

ARRIVAL IN BUDAPEST

Like Paris, Budapest also has its Gare de l'Est (Keleti Pályaud-var), and Gare de l'Ouest (Nyugati Pályaudvar). We were entering the city from the northwest, and arrived at Nyugaty Pályaudvar late that afternoon. At the station we were met by my Aunt Manci and Uncle Arthur. Uncle Arthur's large Buick was waiting for us outside the station. The car, was driven by his chauffeur, and we were all taken to his luxury apartment, where Aunt Ada waited for us with a splendid meal. The tablecloth was of the finest damask, the food was served in Rosenthal tableware and the cutlery was silver. I felt oppressed by the opulent luxury of the apartment and lifestyle of our relatives, and could not stop thinking about the trainloads of people stripped of everything and transported to a destiny which at that time even with the most vivid imagination one could not foresee. The thought of the cattle trucks, into which our friends were probably now being squeezed, made the opulence of our relatives difficult to tolerate. Perhaps it was just the loss of our home, the sleepless night, worry about my father and his border crossing combined with exhaustion that made me feel so miserable and intolerant. After all, our relatives were trying to do the best for us, and despising the luxury of their lifestyle was just as superficial as sneering at poverty.

After our meal I was sent off to bed. The clean, cool sheets and light duvet were an excellent remedy for my fatigued body and mind. My mother stayed with my aunts and uncles to discuss the next arrangements to be made.

Next morning, we had news from my aunt Maryshka that my father was safe in Hungary. He would be taking the train to Budapest and arriving at the same time as we had yesterday. This was brilliant news, and much of our anxiety disappeared. The family would be together and this would make all the difference.

Now accommodation had to be found for us. I naively believed, that this exile would end in a few weeks, and that we would soon return home, but my mother tried to prepare me for a long exile. My relatives were all trying very hard to make things easy for me, but I only felt ungrateful that they were so singularly unsuccessful in making me feel better. My sole consolation was that Uncle Hans was due to arrive soon and bring news from home, from Grandma and others. The agony of not knowing anything about our dearest friends and family was greater then the joy that – for the time being at least – we were safe.

3 Life in Budapest, 1942–43

I would like to be loved,
I am no one's relative or happy ancestor,
nor am I anyone's friend or successor.
I am like every human being,
northern mist secret and concealed,
light and vibrant brilliance that glitters in the distance.
But in this condition I am unable to remain,
so now, I will make an effort and strain
to be revealed, seen and by others perceived.
For, within me there still is this futile longing
to strive for happiness, love and belonging.
(free translation of a poem by Endre Ady, 1877–1919)

DIFFICULT START: TRAINING IN DECEPTION

My relatives obtained some documents for us, which stated that we were Hungarian nationals, Catholics from the newly-occupied northern border territories that were previously part of Czechoslovakia. We had to learn our new names, and assume new identities. Our family name would no longer be Sidon, but Takács. We kept our first names so as to hold onto at least something from our past. We had to try to become other people, to learn as much as possible about the little village we were supposed to come from, about the people we were impersonating, their background, profession, families and friends. This, though very strange and extremely difficult for my parents, was quite easy for me. In fact, I was thrilled to impersonate someone different and mould myself into a new person.

The difficulty for me was that I could not speak Hungarian. Indeed, I presented a real danger to myself and my parents; how could I be a Hungarian girl and not be able to speak the language? This was a serious problem, and I realized that for my own safety and that of my family I would have to learn to speak Hungarian not only well but also very quickly.

A quite spacious two bedroom flat was found and rented for us, in Buda, near the fashionable Gellért Hotel, in what was then called Horthy Miklós Street. The building was quite old and the corridors and staircases dark. We registered in our new names. All apartment houses in Budapest had a most unpleasant feature: a concierge who was really a police informant. The concierge had a flat on the ground floor with a window facing the entrance hall, so someone was always looking out of the little window to watch what was going on, on the lookout for someone to denounce.

Our flat was on the first floor, and to reach it we had to pass a dark, dingy passage. The two rooms and the kitchen were partitioned off from a larger flat. The furniture was old, heavy and neglected, as was everything else in the flat. My mother's attempts to make the place look cheerful were at first not very successful, and a stale, depressing atmosphere permeated the place. But it was the bedbugs and their fearless attacks at night that really plagued us. At first we didn't know why all three of us came up in these red spots on our wrists and temples, and why each morning new spots joined the old ones. We thought that we had some strange disease, but none of us felt really ill. Then my mother asked the landlady what it could be and she laughed and said: 'These are typical bedbug bites. The whole house is infested with them. I will give you a spray and show you how to apply it so you can keep the numbers of these insects under control.' From then on my mother launched a passionate crusade against the bedbugs. It was in the corners of the bed frames where the flat insects retreated after their bloody feast, so the wooden frames were taken apart and sprayed by a foul smelling liquid of strange oily consistency.

My mother spent a lot of energy trying to clear up the place – removing the ingrained grime from the furniture, washing the carpets, lining the drawers in the kitchen cabinets with white paper. But my father and I were so desperately miserable in these shabby surroundings that we did not help very much. We were longing for our old home, the friends we left behind; in other words, our old life. We had no friends in our new life, no interesting work, and I had nothing to occupy me and stimulate my mind. I moped about, not joining in any of the efforts my parents made to settle, just feeling lonely, displaced and shamefully sorry for myself, and this only served to make things worse. In contrast, my mother had the wisdom to keep our situation in perspective. She kept telling me that faced with the other possibility of deportation to Poland, we were lucky to be here and to be together as a family. She set off with great energy to try and make the best of the present situation and create as pleasant a life for the family as possible under the circumstances. In addition to cleaning the flat she bought flowers to cheer it up, which she put into empty milk bottles. To this day I feel ashamed that not only did I not help, but I didn't show my appreciation for all her efforts. I remember how pleased she was with the results and how her blue eyes lit up when on rare occasions my father or I commented that the flat was beginning to feel like home.

To find some outlet for my teenage energy I spent a lot of time daydreaming. It was spring, and the nearby Gellért Hegy (hill) was looking very inviting. Almost every day I took long walks on the Gellért Hegy, but instead of enjoying the lovely spring weather and scenery during these walks I was brooding and wallowing in self-pity. How unfair, I thought, that at the age of 15 I was not allowed to go to school, that I had no friends, knew no young people of my own age. I felt terribly lonely and also guilty that my depression caused pain to my family, who tried their best to keep our lives together. None of the arguments my parents used about our good fortune to have escaped deportations and being still together as a family cheered me up, and although I knew the grief and pain that I caused my parents, I did not try hard enough to change and be more positive. The long walks helped me, however, and I usually came back home a little more refreshed.

One day after such a walk, filled with self-indulgent brooding, I returned home and noticed that our kitchen had indeed become bright and cheerful. I felt ashamed of my self-indulgence, and sad that I had not contributed anything to the transformation of the place. I embraced my mother, and asked: 'Can I do anything to help?' 'Yes, Gerti,' my mother replied, 'I used up all the matches, and I cannot light the gas stove, so could you go out and buy some?' I was taken aback by this, for I couldn't speak Hungarian, and according to my forged papers I was supposed to be a Hungarian country girl who had recently moved to Budapest and could speak no other language. How could I go out to buy anything without giving away the truth? So I protested: 'Mother, you know I cannot go – I don't know how to ask for matches in Hungarian, and everyone will realize that I am a foreigner.' My mother smiled at me, sat down at the table, and said with a mischievous look in her eyes: 'I know, but you have to learn fast, and this is the way to do it. I will teach you what to say, and you will have to repeat the sentence to me until you get it right. So here we go; you enter the shop and say: "*Jó napot kivánok, kérek egy doboz gyufát*" (Good day, please give me a box of matches). Then when they hand you the matches you give them the right amount of money, and say: "*Köszönöm szépen*" (thank you). After that you come home.' My mother had me repeat these few words many times, until she was satisfied that I could say them perfectly, without any accent. She also made sure that I knew the Hungarian words for numbers, so that I would understand the price. After a while, I felt confident enough to go out and buy a box of matches. It had now been three weeks since I arrived in Budapest, and this was the first time that I had dared to go into a shop on my own.

In a way this was a turning point, for the inability to communicate and understand people around me made matters much worse. So although apprehensive, I was really happy to be sent on this errand on this cool, late April afternoon. As soon as I entered the shop however, I realised with horror that although I remembered most of the sentence my mother had taught me, I could not recall the word for 'matches'. Instead of the Hungarian word, only the Slovak and German words kept popping into my memory. I was terribly embarrassed and walked out of the shop to go back home. I told my mother what happened and she said: 'I should have thought of writing it down for you. You could have been reminded of the word for matches by glancing at the paper, and you would have felt more secure and confident. So I will do that now and you just go out and try again.' I went to a different shop, and this time there was no problem; I got the matches and brought them home. From then on, I tried to speak only Hungarian, learning each sentence I wanted to say and practising it until I could say it properly using the right pronunciation. This was a most efficient way of learning and within six weeks I could speak passable Hungarian. Although my pronunciation was good, my vocabulary was limited, but for the country girl that I was supposed to be that did not matter. Gradually, I became quite expert in impersonating a Hungarian country girl. But this training in deception didn't help the fact that I was an uprooted adolescent looking for her own identity.

Being able to speak the language and improving my language skills quickly enough that I was able to read and understand Hungarian literature and poetry did help me though. I became less gloomy and had more interest in life. Yet my loneliness and need for young people's company was so intense that I was prepared to do anything, even take risks, just to spend some time with people of my own age. I didn't tell my parents of my need, but they knew me well enough to understand it and asked my relatives to help.

Some friends of my aunt had children of my age and they arranged for me to meet them. I was excited about the meeting, and thought about what we might talk about or do together. Finally we met at my aunt's flat. They were two 16-year-old boys, well dressed and very neat, who talked about school, clothes, holidays, with not a sign of worry at what was happening in war-torn Europe, yet alone the Jews in German-dominated countries. I tried to find out what they thought about these problems, but they were not interested. I became aware that the difference between them and me was so great that even if we had the time and energy we could never overcome it. The young people I was introduced to were frivolous sons of rich, privileged parents, who had nothing in common with me, a Slovak refugee, and who would rather not know about my problems. They gave me the impression that they blamed us for the situation we were in. They certainly did not seem to believe that the war would ever affect them or interfere with their life, and worse still, they were uninterested in the problems that not only Jews but other people in the world had, as a result of the war. They treated me as an oddity, someone they would rather not know about, and seemed to think that we Slovak Jews brought the persecution onto ourselves by not becoming properly assimilated and part of the Slovak nation. This they believed could never happen in Hungary, where at least the wealthy Jews were properly integrated into Hungarian society and valued members of Admiral Horthy's fascist establishment. When on rare occasions I went out with them, they talked only about their school, about the sports they were involved in, and boasted about their Hungarian friends from aristocratic families. These things were not only meaningless, but also incomprehensible to me. They never asked about me, what it felt like being a refugee, assuming another identity, not being able to go to school, and being completely displaced. They were not interested in social problems either, and I longed to discuss with them topics that had so fascinated me during our discussions in Trnava, for I believed that understanding these problems might help us to deal with the present and the future. I was deeply disappointed by this lack of communication. After a while I no longer wanted to see any of them and preferred to be lonely.

The weather was getting warmer as spring changed into summer. I was painfully aware that I had only one change of clothes and that they were too warm to wear in the summer heat. My mother noticed the problem, and persuaded my aunts to help me with my wardrobe. Thus I was taken to a dressmaker in one of Budapest's most fashionable salons, where my aunts chose some materials and styles for me. The dressmaker took my measurements and arranged a date for me to come back and have the dresses fitted. I got three new dresses, which I loved, and which were far beyond what I had expected. I was delighted that I looked so elegant. Then I was taken to another shop, where we bought jumpers to wear in the evenings, and some new underwear. After each of these successful expeditions, we ended up in a fancy coffee shop, Gerbaud, where I drank the most wonderful hot chocolate and was allowed to choose two cakes. This luxury at a time when most of us European Jews suffered the most awful fate, seemed a truly criminal act, and I had the most terrible feeling of guilt. Sometimes this feeling was so intense that I could not finish eating my cakes, or drinking the chocolate. Often, my thoughts were far away, trying to join my old friends, imagining where they might be. My aunts didn't show that they noticed my detachment. At times I was quite ungracious, even rude to my very generous, loving family. From not eating cakes it was only a short step to not being able to eat anything at all, and this caused great concern to my parents. I lost a lot of weight, my periods stopped and I was very weak.

This was summer 1942. Europe was at war and Hungary was a staunch ally of the then victorious Germans. It seemed incredible that amidst this turmoil the lifestyle of some of the rich Hungarians seemed unaffected by these events. They still enjoyed all the luxuries of life, indulged in eating exquisite meals at famous restaurants, played bridge and had large parties. My uncles and aunts were no exception. It was to me unbelievable that the Hungarian Jews did not want to conceive that there was a real threat for them, their concern focused only on the most immediate problems and they made no preparations for the danger they faced.

My family was concerned about me, for I had been suffering from a serious depression and was obviously sick. To help me to snap out of this, my aunt Manci bought me a season ticket to one of Budapest's most luxurious swimming pools on Margaret Island in Budapest. This was a far cry from the swimming pool in Trnava where Manci taught me how to swim; it was more like a spa, with three different size pools, one of the Olympic size, which had artificial waves at hourly intervals. There were lush lawns, deckchairs, table tennis facilities and food stalls. It was the most wonderful place I had ever seen.

Perhaps Manci thought that the magic of the days in the shabby swimming pool in Trnava might be repeated in this very different luxurious setting on Margeret Island. I was taken there almost every day to swim and sunbathe with my Aunt Manci and her friend Aladár. Manci and Aladár covered themselves in suntan lotion and did a lot of swimming, several laps a day in the Olympic-size pool. They looked tanned and healthy; I, meanwhile, sat in the sun watching the people around me enjoying themselves, swimming, playing table tennis, and couldn't help thinking of my friends. Were they still alive, and if so how much did they suffer? So it was not surprising that all the efforts my family made to improve my state of mind during those hot summer months were not very successful. Although I too was nicely tanned, I became more and more despondent, and was in no better shape then before my visits to the swimming pool. At the time I was quite unaware of the pain and anguish I caused my parents by my behaviour.

It was at the end of the summer, when the swimming pool closed for the winter, that my mother, with her intuitive common sense and understanding of my problems, found a solution.

Financially our family was completely dependent on support we had from my mother's brother, my uncle Arthur.

Neither my mother nor my father was satisfied with this situation, but it was impossible for any of us to get employment, since our papers were forged, and it would have been dangerous. My resourceful mother found some work that could be done at home without any questions being asked; she got commissioned by a shop to knit gloves and scarves, and asked me to help. I was delighted to be asked, and started the work with great enthusiasm. It gave me a feeling of dignity, and kept me busy for several hours a day. Now that I earned some money I felt it right that I should spend some of my 'income' on my education and so French lessons were arranged for me. My mother found a delightful lady who not only taught me French, but also contributed to my education in other ways. She supplied me with books, some of which were banned, and it was through her that I discovered the novels of Romain Roland, and other French novelists. Gradually my usual energy returned, and I began to appreciate my family's efforts to help me over my adolescent misery.

I started to look around for other sources of education. My aunt Manci was often my adviser. She understood my frustration, for she too had been prevented from spreading her wings. When she was 23 she graduated from the University in Bratislava, where she studied philosophy and languages. She was brilliant, and won a scholarship to spend a year in Paris. Unfortunately my father, her older brother and the rest of the family thought it unsuitable for a young girl to live on her own in Paris and didn't allow her to take up the offer. Shortly afterwards she was married off to a much older man and her marriage was unhappy and childless. I think she never quite got over her disappointment at not having been allowed to take up the scholarship in Paris.

Manci found some information about education courses in Budapest and I was present when she pleaded with my parents to allow me to attend some of them. My parents were naturally worried that in view of my illegal status even attendance at such courses might be dangerous, but Manci felt that she could protect me. I attended a most bizarre selection of courses, which had no connection with each other and which I often didn't understand; they ranged from Greek mythology and art history – especially Italian renaissance – to electronic engineering, mathematics and physics.

As time went on the luxurious life of the rich in Budapest was becoming less ostentatious. The Germans demanded food supplies from the Hungarian government and this led to food shortages. For the civilian population, rations for food and other items were introduced. This made it even more complicated for people like us, who had illegal documents and were not properly registered. We had to buy ration books on the black market, and that was yet another danger.

The city was losing its glittering appearance, warnings of air raids had become quite common and complete blackouts were introduced. In night clubs sentimental songs were sung, to entertain Hungarian men drafted into the army.

Russia was at war now, and the Hungarians together with the Italians and Germans were taking part in the attempt to conquer Russia. Rumours of the atrocities committed by these three allied armies in Russia were filtering through, and Hitler's relentless progress deep into Russia was filling us with despair. At this stage, we could not imagine that we would live to see Hitler's defeat; yet in spite of all the gloomy news, my father was always full of optimism and hope.

Throughout the winter of 1942 we always eagerly awaited my uncle Hans's visits. He brought us news from home, and we would talk about those we left behind. We learned that my uncle Karol had been left in peace and had not been deported, because his farm was important for the country's economy and food supply. His wife and two children continued to live on the farm. The same applied to my mother's two sisters and their families, both of whom were married to farmers. But I was always particularly anxious to hear about grandma. Hans reported that she was looked after by a friend and was still in our old house. So our immediate family had not yet been deported.

And then I got a wonderful surprise: Uncle Hans brought

me my ice skates from home. 'Grandma said you would like these now that it is winter,' he told me. He took my arm and said: 'Get your coat and we will go shopping.' I didn't know what he wanted to buy, but I did as I was told. We went to a sports shop, and my uncle bought me a wonderful skating outfit: light blue jumper, navy trousers and a warm woolly hat. Then he took me to the skating rink and watched me skating. When we went home he said to me: 'You were the prettiest girl in that rink.' Though I knew he said it to please me I felt very happy. With all the good news from home, and the pleasure of skating and gliding on the ice, as I used to do every winter before we were forbidden to do so, life seemed to be tolerable.

The winter passed and soon we celebrated the completion of our first year in Hungary. Somehow days that seemed endless in the beginning began to pass more quickly and spring 1943 arrived. We were by now quite well organized. Italian renaissance paintings were my latest hobby and I spent hours in art galleries. My father met several of his acquaintances almost daily in our flat, and we tried to convince ourselves that the turning point of the war was nearing. This was easier to believe now, for it was apparent that Hitler had not managed to invade England, and his Russian campaign was also not likely to be completed soon. My father had great confidence in history repeating itself, and often described events from Napoleon's campaign against Russia, back in the nineteenth century. It is amazing how willing we were to believe these optimistic predictions.

As spring approached, I often took long walks on the hill near our house. During these walks I frequently saw a young man about my own age. We started talking to each other and discovered that we had many interests in common. We both liked poetry and literature and it was good to talk to a person my own age at last about problems that interested me, though I never discussed politics with him. Instead, we talked about Italian renaissance, Dante and love. The young man, András, was a student of literature. He wrote poetry and read his poems to me, which I thought were magnificent. For me the meetings with him were exciting and enjoyable, for he was the only young man in Budapest I knew. We held hands occasionally, but we never kissed, much as I would have liked to have been kissed by him. In spite of the strange times and my unusual problems I was still a teenager who longed for the company of boys and who wanted to be loved. Thus my walks with András to the top of the hill, from where we watched the sprawling city, the Danube and the houses of parliament on the other side of the river, gave me a real thrill and much pleasure. We knew hardly anything about each other; I never told András who I really was or where I lived, and he didn't talk about his family. Yet I felt guilty about deceiving him. Being secretive became increasingly difficult as we grew fond of each other, but still I was too scared of betrayal to risk confiding in him. However, András knew that I didn't go to school, because we often met at times when I should have been there, so he might have been suspicious.

My parents were unaware of my meetings with András. I never told them anything about him, and when I was to meet him I just told my parents that I was going for a walk up the hill. I knew that they would worry that meeting András may be dangerous.

4 Hungarian Detention Camp

We didn't know who had denounced us to the police or why they had suspected us: perhaps our lifestyle didn't fit that of a normal working-class Hungarian family and the concierge noticed that we left home and came back at odd times and had no regular routine. With horror I also suspected that it may I have been the young man András, whom I had befriended during my long walks on the Gellért hill and with whom I had often talked, who had betrayed me. He may have noticed something strange about me and followed me home. It was of course possible that he had denounced us, but I didn't want to believe it. The uncertainty that it could have been my relationship with András that had given us away made me feel guilty. Could I have misjudged him so badly? I will never know.

This is how it happened. One evening at about 10 o'clock we heard a loud knock on our front door. We weren't expecting any visitors and an unexpected knock at that time of night frightened us; we knew immediately that it must be the police. My mother opened the door and saw two uniformed policemen standing outside. One of them was plump and when he took off his hat I noticed he was bald. The other one was thin, tall and severe-looking. They were quite polite, and the bald one asked to be allowed to come in. My mother stepped aside and let them in. Then, of course, they wanted to see our identity papers. My father took the documents out of the drawer of the desk in the living room and handed them to the policemen. They looked at them suspiciously and then the tall one said: 'You'd better come with us to the police station where we can check these papers. We were told that you might be illegal immigrants. Pack a few personal things you want to take with you, because if your identity papers are not in order you will be sent to a detention camp.' By then we knew for certain that we would indeed be sent to a camp; we tried to suppress the feeling of panic and to think calmly about what to do. Again it was my mother who dealt best with the situation. She handed me a holdall and told me to pack sensible things that I might need in a work camp. When I had finished, she checked what I had packed. Then she went on to pack her own and Father's bags. Sadly and apprehensively she looked at my father and added: 'They may not leave us together, we'd better have separate cases.' With that, she took out another suitcase and packed Father's things into one of them and hers into the other. Father was helping her to choose what to take, but I noticed that he was too distressed to care either way. Again I knew that the feeling of inadequacy swamped him: he was unable to take proper care of us, and he couldn't bear it.

We were taken to the local police station, where it was soon established that our documents were forged. After a brief interrogation we admitted this 'crime' and reverted to our true identity. This seemed to be a great relief for my father, who much preferred to be Max Sidon than Max Takács. It even returned some of his usual cheerfulness for a short while. We spent the rest of the night in a small cell, but we were together, and that meant a lot to my father. The next day, however, things changed. In the morning we were taken in a police car to an overcrowded prison somewhere in Budapest. There my father was separated from us and was put in the men's section of the prison, while mother and I were in the women's section. We knew that this was just a temporary detention/prison camp. In each room there were about twenty women sleeping on bunk-beds on straw mattresses. After the first frightening two days, we somehow settled into the routine of this bizarre prison life. Each day we were allowed to spend a few hours in the prison courtyard where we could meet the men and where we saw my father. The courtyard also doubled up as some sort of store, for there were huge drums of heavy cable stored there.

During these 'outings' I met other young Jewish girls and boys, who like us had been picked up by the police. One of the boys, a tall, lanky 18-year-old called Laci, was an enthusiastic chess player. He taught several of us how to play chess and then organized chess tournaments. We made our own chess set, the figures shaped from bread and the chessboard a relatively clean piece of concrete between the drums of cable, which also provided us with some shade. Strangely, in spite of the physical discomfort of the place – which was harder on my parents than on me – the dreadful watery soup and the constant fear that we would be interrogated or taken to some other more horrible place, I found the week in this prison quite interesting. I felt less lonely, and knowing that other young people of my age were coping well with the situation gave me hope and confidence.

We were allowed visitors, and my aunts Manci and Ada came to see us, bringing lots of lovely food. The drab prison surroundings made the contrast between us and them even greater, for they were smartly dressed and we were all grey and dirty. They brought some good news though, and hope, for apparently it was possible to be released if you could find the right connection and someone who could be bribed.

After about ten days in this temporary prison, we were marched to the railway station and herded into a cattle truck, which headed north-east. There was a large camp for illegal immigrants and political prisoners in Ritse, on the border between Hungary and what is now the Ukraine, and that was where we were taken.

The summer of 1943 was extremely hot and the detention camp we were taken to in eastern Hungary was in a barren part of the country. There were no trees or any shade, and the sun beat down relentlessly, drying out soil, animals and people. When my parents and I were taken to the camp, we felt that we would be unable to survive the heat and would die of thirst.

As in the previous prison in Budapest, here too women and men were separated, and my father was taken to the men's section of the camp. I knew that my father would suffer terribly as a result of this separation, and indeed, he became seriously depressed and ill. He had ulcers in his mouth and nose, lost a lot of weight and could not get adjusted to prison life, although the conditions were not really harsh. We met almost every day, and my mother and I tried to lift his spirits during our brief meetings. I still remember how he held onto my hand, when we had to separate, and wouldn't let go of it, saying, 'I really let you down, Gerti, I wish I could have protected you.' He clung to us, and I knew that he felt terribly guilty, though obviously he had done all he could for us. Nevertheless, I did understand him: for him and his family to be put into prison or into a detention camp signified a collapse of the world and its rules as he understood them. He was a very honest, law-abiding citizen, who considered disobeying the law a real crime; and now he and his family were in prison because we had disobeyed the law and tried to live by deception on forged papers. He could not accept that it was not him, but the law that was at fault, and he also felt keenly the fact that he could not protect his family.

When, during our brief meetings, I looked at his handsome face, his large hazel eyes so full of suffering and his stooped walk, I was aware that something irreparable had happened to him and that he would never again be the man he had been before they sent us to prison. The physical discomfort in the detention camp was not great, yet the indignity to his person, the negation of his beliefs, had turned him into a broken man. No longer was he able to cheer us all up with his optimistic forecasts about the outcome of war and the inevitability of Hitler's speedy defeat. So far as he was concerned, it didn't matter any more when the war finished, his world would not survive, and he wasn't certain whether he wanted to live in a world that would replace his. I will never forget those few weeks in the detention camp, when my father gave up the fight for survival.

My mother, on the other hand, adjusted to the new situation much better. In the summer heat on our straw mattresses we were plagued by all sorts of insects. There was no electricity in the camp, but we had candles. There were about ten women to a room, and my mother kept us all awake by organizing us to launch the battle against the biting creatures. Somehow, she got hold of some pins, and we were told to collect the bedbugs with these and then assemble the catch on a piece of paper. Fleas were more difficult to catch, but my mother was very good at it. We had a knitted blanket given to us by a relative before we left, and it was a perfect home for fleas, who settled in the knitted material, but my mother somehow found a way to expel them, I think we were the only room in the entire camp that had relatively few biting insects, and after a while we could sleep quite peacefully.

My mother also made many friends and discovered that someone had playing cards. She organised bridge tournaments, and since she was an excellent bridge player, she usually won them. Most of the women loved and respected her, for she helped them to endure camp life. During the day we had to work – usually digging in the 'garden' or helping in the kitchen – but the evenings were free. Though outwardly my mother seemed strong and adjusted, she suffered greatly because of my father. She tried to encourage him, to reassure him that we were well and to convince him that we needed him. During our meetings with him, Mother always tried to look cheerful and encouraged me to do the same. We knew that the only thing that mattered to my father was our well-being, and we had to make him believe that we were in fact fine. He seemed eventually to accept this and gradually became resigned to our fate.

There were several girls of my age or just a little older in the camp and our evenings together were quite pleasant. As the heat of the day was replaced by the cool evening air, we sat together outside, talking, singing and playing music. One of the girls, Viola, also from Slovakia, had a guitar, which she played well. Accompanied by this she sang wonderful songs to us in her deep, husky voice. She taught us to sing with her, and sitting there singing together we managed to relax in the cooler evening air. The anticipation of these evenings helped us to get through the day. As the dry heat of the day gave way to the cool evening air, even the vast, flat expanse of the Hungarian countryside seemed yielding and pleasant; memories of the heat and merciless sun that had plagued us only a few hours before when we had been working in the fields were forgotten and replaced by a feeling of together-ness and of sharing the same fate. Sharing the same experi-ence with others felt new to us, for we had all lived a lonely life in Hungary before being taken to the detention camp. It was probably because of this hunger for the company of other young people that friendships and trust developed almost instantaneously.

Most of the girls had been sent to Hungary from Slovakia by their parents to stop them from being deported, for the earliest deportations in Slovakia were those of boys and girls between the ages of 16 and 20. Many of the girls in our group had joined various groups of young Jews in Hungary that tried to organize help for the refugees and also provided forged documents for Hungarian young men to avoid being taken to work camps on the eastern front. Viola (the guitarist) and her sister Ibolya came from a small town at the foot of the Tatra Mountains in Slovakia. They had no family in Hungary, but had contacts in one of the organizations that helped and supported Jewish refugees. They were caught, and the Hungarian police were eager to discover the names and addresses of the members of the group that had helped them. Both girls were tortured for fourteen days by the Hungarian secret service, to force them to disclose the names of their friends. They were kept in overheated rooms without being given water or food. When they were thirsty, they were tied to a bench while cold, icy water was dripped onto their forehead, but it never reached their lips. I didn't know whether the torture made them disclose their friends' names, or whether they even knew their friends' real names and whereabouts. After their ordeal the detention camp was a real relief. Ibolya also had a lovely voice, and knew an endless number of songs which she sang with Viola. Later, after she had taught us some of them, we all sang them together.

After the war, when I left Czechoslovakia and spent a year in Denmark, I managed to trace Viola. She was married to a Dane and lived in Jutland. When we met, she told me that she had managed to survive Auschwitz, but that Ibolya had died. Viola was happy with her husband and enjoyed her two children, but could never get over the loss of her parents and Ibolya. We were glad to have our memories of our evenings in the camp in Hungary to remember Ibolya by.

Then there was little Sophie, a young Polish girl who had her violin with her and who played for us. She came from a small Polish town near Krakow and had made her way through Slovakia to Hungary. She talked about the unbearable conditions of the ghetto in Krakow, and the atrocities committed by the Germans in Poland. She and her fiancé had hoped that they would be able to make their way to Palestine through Hungary, but they were caught by the Hungarian police and tortured. Sophie's fiancé died during his torture. After her ordeal, for her also the detention camp was indeed a pleasant place to be. Sophie survived the war and ended up in Israel, where she was originally headed.

Danica was from Croatia, where the overzealous, fascist Croatian militia had rounded up the Jews and Serbs, and shot them into the river that flowed through Zagreb. Danica came from a small village outside Zagreb. Her parents were killed, but Danica somehow managed to escape and to reach Hungary. She was caught as she made her way to Budapest and sent straight to the detention camp, where she was quite satisfied to be alive. I admired her looks – her dreamy dark blue eyes that shone in her tanned face – but I never got to know her well and do not know what happened to her.

I felt I was the most protected and least experienced of all the girls I met in the camp, for all the others fended for themselves alone, without help from parents or relatives. I was also the youngest and I felt delighted to be accepted by the others, who in my eyes were real heroes. I tried to listen carefully to the accounts of their experiences and descriptions of their fate. Perhaps I knew that I should start learning how to face adverse situations independently and make my own decisions. It may sound odd, but these few weeks in the detention camp were the happiest time I spent in Hungary.

Then one day a car arrived along the dusty road. My aunt and uncle, who had somehow managed to arrange our release, came to fetch us. I felt guilty and sad leaving my friends behind. I think my parents and I were the only ones ever to be released from the camp.

Curious to find out how our release was achieved, I asked my uncle, for I knew that he had arranged it. He tried to describe his efforts as clearly as possible.

One of his friends had introduced him to an official in the Hungarian Ministry of the Interior (home office) who dealt with matters of illegal immigrants. My uncle arranged to meet this person and took him out for dinner in a fashionable and very expensive restaurant (Gundel) in the city park. He described in great detail the meeting with this gentleman. After a sumptuous meal and several bottles of expensive wines, paid for by my uncle, my uncle asked his guest how much it would cost to have his sister and her family released on bail. 'Impossible,' shouted my uncle's guest, 'You must understand that we can't release Jews on bail. These people cheat and live here on forged papers. They have to be kept in prison or detention camps.' My uncle reported that after this lecture he ordered another portion of dessert, a wonderful chocolate-covered pancake that was a speciality of the restaurant, and continued the negotiation. 'I know it's going to be expensive, so let's not waste time. Just tell me how much it will cost, and how you want the payment to be made.' The Hungarian official looked serious and said: 'This really is an exception and believe me I am doing it mainly out of friendship for you, not just for money. You helped the friend who introduced us by giving him a loan when he was in trouble, way back, and I can't turn you down, but it will cost a lot of money. I will have to bribe many people, my share will be very small, and my career is at stake. I am really taking an enormous risk to help you.'

My uncle had to get across his point too and added: 'You can consider your career already ruined since it will not be long before Germany and the Hungarian fascist government will lose the war. I did warn you not to join the right-wing Arrow Cross Party led by Mr Szálasy. I am sure that Hitler will put him in power for a short time, but after the war he and his supporters will be in trouble. Now the only thing you can do to help yourself is to have some 'good deeds' on your books, so I am really giving you a chance. Now tell me how much will you charge.' My uncle Arthur was a good business man and shrewd negotiator. '10,000 pengö for the three of them,' muttered the official, 'I will try to make sure then that unless they really misbehave, they will not be tortured. I can't arrange their release quickly, it will take one to two months.' My uncle accepted these conditions. 'You get what you asked for, 3,000 pengö now, another instalment when I can visit my sister and her family in the detention camp and she confirms that you are keeping your word, and finally the last 4,000 pengö when they are released. I am sorry, but now I have to go home, and I guess that you would prefer not to be seen to be driven by my chauffeur in my car.' My uncle paid the bill, which must have been enormous, and drove back home to his luxurious life. His wife, my aunt Ada, arranged a game of bridge, but before leaving he had to tell her of the arrangement he had made. My father Max was her brother, they were very close, and she also loved me very much.

I can imagine that my uncle Arthur often recalled the dusty village that was his and my mother's home. He was the oldest of the thirteen children, and always felt protective towards his siblings, particularly his youngest sister, my mother, whom he adored. He always talked with great affection about her curly blonde hair and large blue eyes. He admired her sharp intelligence, and enjoyed her wit and sense of humour. He would have given anything to have her better educated, but at the time he couldn't afford it. Yet she did well. By marrying my father she had a lovely partner, a decent, honest person, perhaps too nice to cope with the things to come. My uncle was very fond of me too, and I guess he was perhaps the only one in our family who understood how very tough, even ruthless, I could be and was not misled by my innocent, gentle looks.

We were taken back to our old flat, but this time we had our own legal documents with our own names. The only condition of our release was that father had to report every month to the police.

5 On the Run Again!

Our flat hadn't changed, but life was getting increasingly more difficult. With the failure of Hitler's Russian campaign in the east, shortages of food and other articles were becoming more obvious. Rationing was introduced and for articles that could be obtained without rations there were long queues. The winter still held its grip on the city: it was cold and the streets looked grey under heavy skies. We were wrapped up in our warmest clothes as we stood for hours waiting for our turn to get some food. Whispers could be heard in the queue: 'Today they promised to have Emmenthal cheese.' Another woman: 'But cheese doesn't keep long, it gets dry very quickly.' Advice came from behind: 'You can keep it fresh if you wrap it in a wet clean cloth, then it will stay moist.' I still remember this advice, which often came in useful. Indeed, on that day Emmenthal was for sale and I got my share and proudly brought it home. Nevertheless, if you had lots of money it was possible to buy almost anything on the black market, so some people always had plenty of supplies.

Hitler was putting pressure on the Hungarian government for more troops and food supplies. In addition, the German government was getting impatient with Admiral Horthy's reluctance to allow the deportation of Hungarian Jews. Yet winter 1943–44 was for some Hungarians – and this included most Jews – still deceptively peaceful.

BABY'S STORY

I was 17 years old, restless for the company of young people and frustrated by sitting at home. I wanted to take the first opportunity to find a job and leave home. Finally just such a chance arose. A distant cousin of my father's, called Baby (though she was quite grown up), had three small children and wanted someone to help her to take care of them. I went to see her in her house in the Buda Hills. It was a clear morning, and when I reached the house the view of the city was stunning; I could see the Houses of Parliament, the Danube and most of Pest. Baby's house was untouched by the ugly events that surrounded us. The tennis court was well kept, the swimming pool covered up for the winter. The paintwork – a combination of lime green and white – was in perfect condition. I rang the bell and was shown in by a uniformed maid. My cousin Baby, who was waiting for me, welcomed me. She put her arms around me and planted a kiss on my cheek. She had a lovely, joyful face, with mischievous blue eyes, and was bursting with energy. I took to her immediately. Then I met the children that I would have to take care of: Maria, who liked to be called 'Mayo', aged 8; Daisy, 6; and Bencze, just 9 months old. The children were much more uninhibited then I had expected, and the house had a happy, open atmosphere. My cousin Baby seemed to like me and offered me the job, explaining that in return for taking care of the three children I would be given a small room to myself, all the food I wanted and some pocket money. Supervision of Mayo's and Daisy's homework was also among my duties.

Thus I settled in my cousin's luxurious villa in the hills of Buda. Apart from the tennis court and swimming pool I noticed many other privileges that the rich seemed to enjoy. It was strangely incongruous that even at a time like this, when Europe was in the midst of such turmoil, with so much death and suffering, people with lots of money still had the most extraordinary privileges and indulged in peculiar whims. For example, arrangement of the bedrooms amused me, and I couldn't understand the reason for it. Baby and her husband Imre had separate bedrooms, but their beds were either side of a partition. This partition was designed so that on pressing a switch, it moved and the two beds were then adjacent to each other. I still remember my total consternation when first I saw this trick and it wasn't until much later that I thought that this was not such an entirely foolish idea, particularly if one of the partners snored.

During my stay with Baby and her family I learned many new things that influenced my thinking. Baby led a very active cultural life, and ran a sort of 'salon' where interesting people met and discussed musical events, new books and new ideas. I was often given tickets to the opera and went almost every week. Since many of the performers were frequent visitors of Baby's 'salon', I could discuss with them later anything about the performance that I didn't understand.

Perhaps the most interesting people in Baby's circle were a group of psychoanalysts, in particular Emi Pickler and her friends. They discussed Freud, Jung and problems of the human psyche. Somehow, for a 17-year-old girl, the understanding of one's self and the roots of one's feelings, desires etc. was still important even under those very strange and artificial circumstances.

Baby and I became very fond of each other, and I had tremendous admiration for her. She was a very clever woman who used her privileges well. After I had put the children to sleep I often sat at the foot of her bed and we talked for hours. There were many issues that we disagreed on. I was at the time an enthusiastic Socialist, and argued with Baby that this was the only solution for creating a dignified, just society. Baby's argument against it was not always concerned with principles. She was honest enough to admit that in her position, as a rich upper-middle-class person, socialism was not a desirable system. But she also argued that socialism was not the solution, because various aspects of human nature

63

would always prevent it from achieving its goal. However, our disagreements did not diminish my admiration and love for her.

These discussions were purely theoretical. Baby, unlike many others at the time, saw all too clearly that the days of the Hungarian Jews were numbered, and that we were heading towards much more difficult times. She had in fact prepared for the worst and made reliable arrangements for all of her family to be hidden by one of her many Hungarian friends when the time came. (Baby and her family survived the war and the persecution by the communist Hungarian government that followed. Somehow, after the 1956 uprising, the family managed to emigrate to the US and settled in Los Angeles.)

The few months of the winter of the year 1943–44 seemed to go by very quickly. I saw my parents every weekend and was saddened by the change in my father, who became more gloomy every week until there was little we could do to cheer him up. In spite of the fact that the fortunes of war had really turned in favour of the Russians, and our return to Trnava seemed likely, my father could not believe what was happening, and like a plant left without water and nourishment for too long, deprived of his habitual optimism he could not recover his spirit. He was worried about us, and the belief that he might be able to help us was perhaps the only thing that kept him going. It was increasingly hard for my mother to try and keep his gloomy moods at bay since she too was losing her fighting spirit.

SPRING 1944

The spring saw an escalation of the disagreement between the Hungarian government and the German Nazi demands for a speedy 'final' solution to the Hungarian Jewry. The preparations for the extermination of the Hungarian Jews in Auschwitz were nearly complete and all that was needed now was to organize the round-up and transport of the victims to the appropriate site, yet Admiral Horthy was still dragging his feet. The political turmoil in Hungary escalated. Some time in the middle of March, Admiral Horthy was summoned by Hitler. In his absence, the Germans occupied Hungary and installed a pro-German government under the leadership of Döhme-Stójay, former Hungarian ambassador to Berlin. People with liberal views as well as many Jews were arrested, and we knew that our days in Budapest were numbered. This was immediately apparent as the new regulations came into being.

It was a lovely, mild spring day when my father came to see me in Baby's house. I was in my small room, and when he entered I tried to persuade him to come outside for a walk. He refused, and sat down on my bed. He looked at me with love and affection and a forlorn expression in his eyes. 'You must forgive me that I have always made the wrong decisions, and brought you into danger. Your mother wanted us to emigrate, but I had too much trust in my fellow citizens, and didn't believe that they would let us down, and now it is too late.' I stood up from the bed, took his head into my hands and kissed him. I knew he was saying 'goodbye' to me, but I didn't want to believe it. 'Dad, you have been wonderful to me, you gave me so much love, pleasure and will to live. You mustn't blame yourself for trusting people, trusting our future. You can't live without trust.' He had tears in his eyes when he said: 'Gerti, please remember all the good times we had together. Tomorrow I have to go and report to the police, I do not know what will happen. I can't stay with you any longer, I have to go home and discuss things with your mother.' Then he got up, hugged me and left the room. Somehow I knew that this was the last time I would see him.

Later I heard that my mother and all his friends tried to dissuade him from going to the police and to go instead into hiding, but somehow he thought it best for all of us for him to report, another example of his misplaced respect for any law however 'unlawful' and his confidence that by obeying the law even of a warped fascist society, all would be well. Most people of his generation could not see that the rules and laws of an unlawful society should be defied.

My feeling of loss when he left was justified, since my premonition that this was the last time I was to see him proved accurate.

Together with the German army that marched into Hungary to take over control, a special detail headed by Adolf Eichmann also entered Hungary. There were rumours that now things would be tough for Jews and that strict measures against Jewish refugees would now be taken.

My mother, still hoping for my father's return, waited all day that 1 April, and all night. She was worried and scared. Later she told me that when the doorbell rang a few days later at 7 o'clock in the morning, she ran to the door expecting my father to be there, though she knew it was unlikely, for he had the keys to the house and could let himself in. Instead of my father, there was a stranger who apologized for calling so early. My mother was suspicious, but when the man said he was bringing a message from my father, she invited him into the flat. The stranger introduced himself as András Fekete. My mother described him as a kindly-looking man of about 60, with sparkling blue eyes. He explained that he had been at the police station at the same time as my father, but was released later because he was not a Jew but a political dissident. He told my mother that he had spoken to my father after he had been told that he would not be released. He reported to my mother that my father had trusted him, and had given him her address so that he could give her a message. The message was that my mother and I should disappear. Apparently, if we stayed in our flat, the police would come and collect us. My father thought we ought to move fast, get new forged papers and go into hiding immediately. The 'messenger' refused the drink my mother offered him and left quickly. As always in this sort of situation, my mother was not certain whether András the messenger was genuine, or whether he was an informer, but for some reason decided to trust him. In any case, she accepted the fact that it was important for us to move fast.

She acted immediately, phoning my Aunt Manci to discuss what to do. It was decided that I should be moved from my cousin's house. Manci came straightaway to see me there and to tell me what had happened. I wasn't surprised at the news. Now, I longed to be with my mother, and to share the grief with her, and help to solve whatever problems we would now have to face. I told Manci that I would get ready immediately.

I was very agitated and Manci tried to calm me down. She told me not to rush things, and suggested that she would come back for me with a friend and pick me up by car. She had already found accommodation for us, a small house quite far from where we were staying, on the outskirts of Budapest, which we would need a car to get to.

Then I went to see Baby to tell her what had happened and that I had to leave immediately. Baby was understanding and gentle and tried to comfort me, for she saw that beneath my calm exterior I was very distraught.

She took me in her arms and told me that she had known for some time now that their days in their home were also numbered and that they would soon have to go into hiding. There were rumours everywhere that Hungarian Jews were now to be rounded up and deported. Nevertheless, with her usual optimism she gave me a big smile and said: 'This war will end soon, and then we will all get together again. I am certain that you will survive, and so will we. Determination to do so is the first battle.' Then we went together to Bencze, the baby boy I had helped to look after, and I said goodbye to him. I knew I would miss him. The other two children were at school, and Baby said she would say goodbye to them for me. I packed my few possessions and was ready to leave. I was sad to go, not only because I was attached to the family and felt that their home was mine too, but also because I knew somehow that their world, which I had enjoyed for several months, would be irretrievably lost in the turmoil of the war. In addition, in spite of Baby's confidence and apparent awareness of the danger I knew that they were vulnerable and not well prepared for things to come. I was worried, but fortunately wrong to fear that I might not see them again.

I left the house, Baby, the children and the few months of peace I had had there with a feeling of great gratitude for the short interval of happiness that I had enjoyed.

Manci and her friend Aladár were waiting for me outside the villa in Aladár's Buick. I sat down in the car and Aladár put my small suitcase into the boot of the huge car. Then we drove off to our new hiding place. When we arrived, my mother was already there with the few belongings she had taken from our old flat. Our new accommodation was a small house just on the outskirts of Budapest, surrounded by a delightful garden that had many fruit trees.

Our next task was to obtain new forged papers as quickly as possible, and one of my mother's friends, a Slovak refugee, arranged this. For a large sum of money our new surname became Takács again. We kept our first names, for the fewer changes there were and the fewer lies we had to memorize, the less likely we were to make mistakes. Thus my full new name was Takács; I was a Catholic and came from Diószeg, a village on the Slovak–Hungarian border. Just in case we would be questioned, we tried to become as true to our assumed identity as possible. We revised the few Catholic prayers, the new testament, etc. that we had learned when we first came to Hungary. We could recite 'Hail Mary' in Hungarian with real expertise, knew what to do during mass and how to behave both outside and inside a Catholic church. We hoped that we would be able to stay in Budapest, find out where my father was and keep in touch with him and the rest of our family in Hungary. This was not to be.

One day in late May the decision was made for us. It was a beautiful spring day, and I was in the garden, high up in the cherry tree picking the few ripe cherries I could find, when a man appeared at the gate. I didn't recognize him, but my mother knew him and took him into the house to talk to him. His name was Ernest and he told us that Manci had given him our address, for she knew that he was a good friend of my father's and she wanted him to tell us the news he had for us by himself. He knew my father's brother's son-in-law Fiala, who was also a Slovak refugee in Budapest. I didn't know much about Fiala, for I was too young back in those days in Trnava to hear or understand the discussions about family problems. Later, my mother explained to me that my father's oldest brother, Uncle Karol, had two children, Rose and Martin. Rose longed to have a husband and couldn't find one. At some stage this Fiala appeared on the scene and showed an interest in her, and Rose fell madly in love with him. The family was quite upset by this, because Fiala had quite a disreputable character, and was rumoured to be just after Rose's money, so Rose's father didn't want to allow Rose to marry him. However, it was too late – Rose became pregnant and was desperate to marry Fiala. Everthing happened quite quickly, and Fiala got a large sum of money that was part of Rose's dowry. Then in 1942 the deportations came. While Fiala was hiding with some friends, he left Rose and their baby daughter to be picked up by the Nazis and sent to Auschwitz, where they disappeared without trace. Fiala then took all the money and left for Hungary, where he was living under a false identity and making a lot of money on the black market. Through his contacts with a group of other Jewish crooks, he was always in touch with the Hungarian authorities in power, and they used him to give information about Jewish refugees.

We had heard about him from our friends, and tried to avoid him throughout our years in Hungary. He tried to keep in touch with my aunts, and pretended to be deeply grieved by the fate of his wife and daughter, though rumour had it that he had deliberately arranged their deportation so that he would get rid of them, and use the money as he pleased.

My parents didn't trust Fiala and were suspicious that he was an informer, so when Ernest told her that this was indeed the case, she wasn't suprised. Ernest told my mother that unobserved, Fiala had followed Manci to our new hideout. Apparently he had then boasted about this during a conversation with other refugees and Ernest had overheard it. Fiala believed that if he reported Jews in hiding he would be spared and Ernest felt that he would almost certainly report us to the police. He urged my mother to leave Budapest as soon as possible. When Ernest had gone, my mother called to me to come down from the cherry tree. We phoned Manci and other relatives and they all agreed that we had to leave as soon as possible.

We packed a few things, as much as we could comfortably carry, and were ready to head towards the Hungarian–Slovak border to return to Slovakia, where rumour had it, the round-up of Jews had stopped.

6 Spring and Summer 1944

Our last night in Budapest was spent in a flat of a friend of my Aunt Manci. We were afraid to stay in our little house outside Budapest or in any place that belonged to our family. The next afternoon we took a train to the border town Diószeg, where my Aunt Maryshka still lived. She sent a friend to the station with some food and drink, but did not dare to come herself, for she was scared that it might be dangerous to be seen at the station.

My mother and I had vivid memories of crossing the border from Slovakia to Hungary two years ago, and well remembered the tricks the guide had used, such as waiting silently for the guards to finish patrolling the place where we wanted to cross the border. We felt confident that we could retrace the route without a guide.

We waited until it got dark and then, in the middle of a dark spring night, the same as that one almost exactly two years before, when we had crossed the border from Slovakia to Hungary, my mother and I retraced our steps across the border, this time in the opposite direction. We arrived before dawn at Sered and waited on the outskirts for daylight before entering the small town. We then took a bus to Bratislava. We moved with great caution, for we had no Slovak identity papers. Fortunately, somehow, security was very lax, and no one asked us any questions, probably because we looked so ordinary, as though we were local citizens.

NEWS ABOUT TRNAVA

It seemed to me as though I had been away a lifetime, not just for two years. Bratislava was now to me a foreign city and everything I used to know and like about it was unfamiliar. Even the old city no longer appealed to me. I felt the whole time a premonition of danger and was scared of being so close to our home in Trnava.

We went to see my Aunt Olga, who had stayed in her old flat in an apartment block by the banks of the Danube. I was not particularly fond of Olga. She was a rather spoiled and hysterical woman. As a young girl she had what was thought to be an incurable illness but luckily she had recovered. Nevertheless, everyone in the family pampered her. When she met her future husband Hans, who was not Jewish, and decided to marry him the family agreed to this without hesitation. With anyone else this would have been unthinkable. A Jewish girl from a good family to marry a Christian was most unusual. Yet, as it turned out, Hans was not only a loving and attentive husband to Olga but was also devoted to our family. He had played a pivotal role in our rescue, and when in 'exile' gave us all his support. His untimely death a few months previously had been a terrible blow to all of us, but before he died he tried to make sure that Olga, and my grandma, Jeanette, who moved in with her, were well looked after and reasonably safe. Seeing my grandma after all this time was the greatest pleasure and treat I had had for years.

But I could tell Olga was worried about having us there, and I understood why. She told us that she would leave us with Grandma and go and see a friend who usually had rooms to let. Then we could move there the same day. My mother was especially grateful to Olga for seeing to these practicalities, and we were pleased to let her go on errands on our behalf. I was particularly pleased to be alone with Grandma.

The two difficult years had taken their toll on her, and she had aged incredibly fast. She told us about what had gone on at our home after we had left to escape to Hungary. 'When you didn't report at the office where they registered the Jews to be deported, two men from the Hlinka guard (the Slovak equivalent of the SS) came to the house in their black uniforms and boots and asked me where you were hiding. I said of course that I didn't know and that I was very upset when everyone disappeared and I was left alone in the house. I think I put on a good show – I cried and complained that you had left me there alone and hadn't told me where you were going. Maybe they believed me, for in spite of a lot of shouting and threatening me with various punishments if they discovered that I was lying, they left me alone in the house. I wanted to take some of your things to our friend Pavelka and others, for them to keep for you for when you returned, but the house was being watched and I didn't dare to do anything.'

Next day Karol came from his farm. He was exempt from deportation because he was an 'economically useful Jew': his farm produced much needed grain and other agricultural products. But he was devastated by the break-up of the family. Uncle Max had died peacefully before deportation could destroy him, but Karol's son, his daughter and her baby were threatened. He told me that he had found an asylum for mentally handicapped people and that he would have to send his son Martin there, for there he stood a better chance of escaping deportation. He also said that he had found a hiding place for his daughter Rose, her husband and their three-month-old baby girl. But he was worried about them, for Rose was not very bright and couldn't understand what was happening, so she was putting everyone in danger by not staying hidden. 'Karol is still on his farm and doing quite well.' Grandma stopped talking for a while, and looked at us with joy. We had still not told her much about ourselves, but we had to tell her where my father was, and it was hard to do this without getting her worried.

Olga had a maid, Maria, a rather plain, colourless girl about 20 years old, and she brought us some cold sandwiches and tea. She eyed us with great interest but didn't talk to us. For some inexplicable reason I felt uncomfortable in her presence. Grandma then continued the account of our family's fortunes. 'Olga and Hans were very good to me. Shortly after you left, they came to pick me up, told me to pack a few of my personal possessions and moved me here to Bratislava. I have been with them ever since, and Hans has somehow managed to keep me safe. In a way it was good that I was here, for when Hans died few months ago, of a massive heart attack, I was able to help Olga. But neither of us have got over the loss of Hans. We grieve for him, and he will never be forgotten by our family.'

I wanted to know what happened to our house. I didn't really care, I was just curious. 'As soon as I left,' grandma said, 'Simončič, our shop assistant and then owner of our shop, moved in with his family – his wife, your friend Marushka, and his son – a real good-for-nothing lad, who goes round beating up Jews and their friends. I don't know anything else, except that he has closed down our shops because he works full time for the local branch of the Hlinka guard. Trnava is a very different place now – there are hardly any Jews, or trade, apart from the market.'

Grandma then told us also about some other members of the family, my mother's two sisters Kornelia and Yeti. They were both married to farmers and so were exempt from deportation as economically important persons. They stayed in Trnava, but as I was well aware, Kornelia's children were in Hungary and Yeti's three daughters were somewhere abroad, in England or Australia or Hungary. It was good news that at least some members of our family were still alive. With the fortunes of war having now turned and the defeat of fascism seemingly inevitable, I felt confident, unfortunately too soon, that some of us might survive.

Although we were exhausted and had not slept all night, my mother and I didn't want to stay in Olga's flat and endanger her and Grandma. Yet, we had nowhere else to go. Just as we were wondering where to put our heads down for a nap,

Olga returned. 'I've got good news. I've found a small one bedroom flat for you. It's not in a nice area, but it's clean and quite well-furnished and equipped. So I hope you don't mind that I rented it for you,' she said. My mother and I were delighted and ready to go. Olga gave us the keys and the address of our new flat and told us how to find it. She quite rightly said that it was better if she did not accompany us, in case someone was watching her flat.

Exhausted and hardly able to walk, we somehow managed to reach our destination, which was indeed in a very neglected, poor part of Bratislava.

The flat was simple, clean and comfortable. There was one small bedroom, a kitchen and a living/dining room. A large wooden table with two drawers at each end stood in the middle of the dining room. Two chairs were tucked under the table and the gas cooker in the kitchen was clean and ready to use.

Grandma had given us some dried camomile for tea, some milk and some biscuits. Mother heated some water and made us a cup of 'tea', but I could not stay awake to drink it and went into the bedroom, where the beds were made up and the sheets clean. I didn't even undress, just collapsed on the bed and fell into a deep sleep.

I woke up late next morning, and realised that my mother must have gone out shopping, for there were fresh rolls and butter on the table and a pot of ersatz coffee. It seemed wonderful to have another home, albeit temporary. Both my mother and I were sad that my father was not with us, but neither of us said anything and instead tried to conceal our sadness from each other.

I felt rested and ready to face the problems of our new existence. We discussed what to do, and the first priority was to obtain new forged papers. I knew from our Slovak friends in Hungary that there were several young men from Trnava living in Bratislava, who were exempt from deportation because of their important jobs. I thought that they could help us to find out how to get forged papers. One of the young men was Josef Weiss, who used to come occasionally to our discussions on the meadow when we were still at home in Trnava. I always liked him, he was efficient and quiet. We were told that he and his brother Dove were members of an underground Zionist organization that had a well-developed network which provided help to people like us.

I telephoned my Aunt Olga, and asked to meet her in a quiet spot in a park. She came, but said that she knew nothing about Josef or his brother, and that she did not want to get mixed up with this. Back at the flat I told my mother about Olga's response. She felt confident that Grandma was likely to know someone who could lead us to Josef. Later in the evening, my mother went to see Grandma. When she returned, she told me that Grandma had given her the address of a friend from Trnava who used to give us religious instruction in our Jewish primary school, and that this man, Mr Mehl, would probably be able to help.

YET ANOTHER IDENTITY

Next morning, my mother and I went to find Mr Mehl. He lived near the synagogue, and was among the few Slovak Jews who had not been deported because he was a member of the Jewish Council. In Slovakia as everywhere else, the Jewish Council was used by the Germans to help to round up the Jews and was kept functioning until the last Jew had been deported, including the members of the Council. But on that spring day in April 1944, Mr Mehl was still in his flat. He was pleased to see us, and gave us a warm welcome. He remembered me and recalled that at the age of about 7 I was extremely religious and wanted to observe every detail of the rules that were part of the Jewish religion. After a brief conversation, Mr Mehl told us where to find Josef. He worked in an office that recorded and kept careful statistics on venereal diseases. He was a very important person.

We said goodbye to Mr Mehl and went to see Josef, whose

office was just around the corner. I was really excited and looking forward to seeing one of my old friends again.

The office where Josef worked was in a lovely art nouveau house, and the inside was well kept and attractive. Josef did appear to have an important job and had an office to himself. Since no one had warned him of our visit, he was taken by surprise and was genuinely pleased to see us. He looked well, and as he got up from his chair to walk towards us, I noticed that he was very well dressed, in a smart suit. He shook hands with my mother, and gave me a great hug. Both of us laughed and joked as though we didn't have a worry in the world. He knew from other friends that we had gone to Hungary, but was not surprised to see us back, for after the extreme right-wing government took over Hungary, many Slovak Jews were returning. Josef indicated that he didn't want us to discuss the real reason of our visit in his office, and he suggested that we should meet for coffee in the afternoon, in the Carlton coffee bar. This suited us, since we had a few errands to make and wanted to get settled in our flat.

We met in the Carlton coffee bar as arranged. The Carlton used to be the smartest restaurant and coffee bar in Bratislava, and was the traditional meeting place for businessmen as well as ladies of leisure, for afternoon coffee. It was another art nouveau building and the inside decorations were also in an art nouveau style. I remembered coming here when I was about 9 years old with my father and meeting my father's brother Sándor, who used to live in Bratislava. Then it appeared to me to be the grandest place I had ever seen, with burgundy drapes and matching carpets. The chairs were also upholstered in a material to match and were soft and comfortable to sit in. The wooden tops of the little coffee tables were polished and so shiny that you could see your reflection when you bent over them. They stood gracefully on gilded, curved, elegant legs that matched those of the chairs. The people in the room had been smartly dressed, talking softly to each other. Now, on entering the same room, it looked like a completely different place. Everything was shabby and old, the carpets and upholstery worn, the tables scratched and damaged. An unpleasant smell of cheap tobacco and beer added to the impression of decay. The coffee bar was full and the appearance of the people who sat at the tables matched the appearance of the room. Most of them were shabby, even dirty, and talked in loud voices, shouting at each other and making obscene gestures that produced fits of laughter. Nevertheless, the atmosphere was relatively carefree, considering that we were at the end of the most horrible war in history.

My mother and I spotted a table with four chairs tucked away in a corner and sat down. The waitress came and we ordered tea. Even before we got the tea, we spotted a young girl who was looking around, obviously searching for someone. She approached us and asked whether we were Josef's friends. Then she told us that she would take us outside to Josef, because he was not allowed into the coffee bar, on account of being Jewish.

After finishing our tea and paying for it, we met the girl just outside the Carlton. She introduced herself as Julia and said that she was helping Josef and the others. I didn't quite understand what sort or help she might be providing, apart from delivering messages. However, I realised that she was ideally suited for running such errands. She was a small, blonde girl, about 18 years old (my age), who was as inconspicuous as a little mouse.

She told us that we would have to visit Joseph's apartment where he lived with his brother. The apartment was in a house on the outskirts of Bratislava and we would have to take the tram. When we arrived, he welcomed us, gave me another big hug and kiss and shook hands with my mother. Before mentioning our request, he told us about various Jewish people from Trnava – who had been deported, and when. His parents, sister and her husband were deported in May 1942, shortly after we left, and Josef went with his brother Dov to Bratislava, where the Zionist organization of which they both were members found them jobs classified as important, so that they were spared. No one heard anything from the deported Jews, and the employees of the Judenrat (Jewish Council) tried to calm everyone by saying that no news was good news, and that most of the people taken away were in work camps. Josef did not believe this. His friends in the Zionist organization had contacts with Polish Zionists and they had heard rumours that most of the Slovak Jews deported that spring had been exterminated. But there was no reliable news, only rumours, and we all wished we knew the truth.

After discussing these horrifying events, Josef asked: 'Where is Max, why is he not with you? I used to like him a lot, he was always so encouraging and optimistic.' My mother told him what happened to my father, and finally Josef got to the point and said: 'I guess I know what you need from me. You will have to have forged papers and assume the identity of Aryan Slovak women. Actually you are in luck, because just before the Russian army marched into eastern Slovakia, a friend of mine managed to steal a bunch of empty birth certificates and empty identity card forms from the registry with the stamp of the village that is now occupied by the Russians. If we use those and make a good job of filling in your new name and so on these documents should be perfect, because no one can check whether they're genuine.' I was beaming with joy; having good papers gave one a great degree of freedom and would allow me to move about or even get a job.

'Will we have to chose a new name?' I asked: 'What do you suggest we call ourselves?' He looked at us, and after a while said: 'Would Jurkovič appeal to you? Many people in eastern Slovakia have names quite similar to Russian or Ukrainian names, and Jurkovič is quite a common name in that area.' Both my mother and I thought that this was quite a good name. We kept our first names, even though Gerti was an unlikely name for a girl from eastern Slovakia. We did not change our date of birth either, because that would have been just something else to memorize. Josef took down all the details. 'It will take about four days to have your papers ready, so can you return here in four or five days? I'd like to have an address where I can reach you, in case I need more information.' We gave Josef our address, and I noticed that he didn't write it down. I guess it was safer for him to just memorize it. Finally he said: 'I'd like you to come to the Carlton coffee bar in four days' time at about 4 o'clock. I might have something for you then.' Before we left, he cautioned us to be careful moving about without any documents, and said we should stay at home until we could collect the papers. Then he looked at me and said: 'Gerti, no one would guess that you are Jewish with your blonde hair and blue eyes. Would you like to work with our organization? We need people who can get jobs in companies and have access to a typewriter and other office facilities. I think when you have your papers you'll be able to get an office job and occasionally help with our work.' I was delighted; at last I would be able to do something for other people instead of being on the receiving end all the time. I couldn't wait to start, though my mother was worried about my getting involved.

We didn't go to see my aunt and my grandma, because we were worried about being followed. My Aunt Olga knew that I loved reading and gave me a nice big book, Romain Roland's *Jean Christophe*. That was a real treat. I thought it was wonderful, and spent most of the next four days reading it. Finally the time came to go and get our new identity. We went as arranged to meet Josef outside the Carlton coffee bar. He wasn't there, but we met the young girl we had met before. She handed us an envelope, saying that it contained our birth certificates and that Josef suggested we now apply for identity cards. She told me that when we presented these documents to the office where they issue identity cards we would get genuine, not forged, identity documents. Since the birth certificates had come from a village that was now occupied by the Russians, the authorities could not check whether or not they were genuine. The girl also told us that Josef wanted me to get in touch with him when our papers were sorted out.

So now we were Josefine and Gerti Jurkovič from a small village in eastern Slovakia. Yet again we had to memorize the

80

background of our identity, before going to the police to get our identity cards. It took a few days to get everything ready; we needed photographs and perfect knowledge of our assumed background. Then we went to the local police station, where they issued identity cards. We looked rather bedraggled and claimed that we had fled to Bratislava from our village because we were scared of being occupied by the Russians. There were many genuine refugees applying for documents at the office, probably people involved in the fascist Hlinka guard, who were truly afraid to stay in their home when the Russians liberated it, so we had little difficulty in getting our genuine identity cards.

GETTING A JOB

Now that we had our papers we could move about with more confidence, and I went to see Josef, hoping he would have some work for me. Josef told me to wait for him outside his office; he was ready to leave and we could talk on the way to his home. I didn't have to wait long before he joined me. He asked me what type of work I could do, and I told him about the secretarial course I had done in Trnava, when I had learned to type and do some shorthand. He said that this was just what was needed, and he knew of a removal company that was looking for a junior secretary. If I wanted, he could arrange an interview with the manager as soon as possible. I was very doubtful whether I would get the job, however, because although I remembered some of the things I had learnt, my shorthand skills were almost non-existent. Still, I thought I might give it a try, and Josef had told me that for their organization access to a typewriter and a well-equipped office would be important.

My interview was arranged for two days later. I bought a book on shorthand in a bookstore and peered at it day and night for two days, but by the interview I could only write shorthand at about the same speed as ordinary writing. I decided that my good memory would have to compensate for my lack of skill in shorthand and arrived at the interview feeling rather shaky.

The office was in a large, drab looking building. My interviewer – my boss if I got the job – was a young, handsome man who tried to put me at ease. He called in a young woman, smartly dressed and friendly, who said that she was in charge of the secretaries in the company. She said she would give me a simple test in typing and shorthand. First, she told me to format and type a simple business letter. I had little difficulty in doing that, since both my spelling and writing ability was good. I was quite pleased with what I produced. Next she dictated a text, which I had to take down in shorthand and then type. I was so nervous that I was trembling all over. She dictated a text of what I presumed had been a contract. I had my pad on my lap, a pencil in my hand and I scribbled as fast as I could in a sort of code that only I could understand. Fortunately the text was quite short, only about two pages, and my memory served me well, for even though I could not decipher all the things I had written in my code, I did remember the text well enough to be able to transcribe it accurately. I think the young woman liked me, for she must have noticed that my shorthand was not that of a professional, and yet she smiled at me after reading my transcript and even praised me, much to my surprise. There was a bit of difficulty over my school certificates, confirmation of my qualifications and lack of references, though I did truthfully say that this would be my first job. When I produced my birth certificate and identity card, and span a sob story of how we had to flee the Russians in a hurry and were unable to take anything with us, there were no further questions. I was offered the job and was told to start as soon as possible.

My boss Martin was a pleasant person, with a good sense of humour and a sceptical view of the fascist Slovak government. If he suspected me of anything else but incompetence at shorthand he never said anything to me. I acted as his personal secretary, had to take down (by shorthand) letters he dictated, type them, take them to him for signature and then send them off. I often changed the text, for his style was not always to my liking, and most of the time he was impressed by the changes I made. I had a key to the office and the building and when I asked him whether I could use the typewriter to type some of my private correspondence in the evenings after office hours, he had no objection. Thus, Josef and his friends had the access to a typewriter that they wanted.

Josef introduced me to some other members of the group, his brother Dov and my old friend from Trnava, Jan. All of them appeared to have been officially employed, but their main work was to produce and distribute forged papers. Thus my typewriter was used to complete various forms – birth and marriage certificates, exemptions from army service, medical certificates and travel permits. Josef also asked me to hide some empty forms in an easily accessible place. He gave me a parcel of them and I taped it to the inside of the kitchen table in our flat. As it turned out that was a fatal mistake. But at the time I was thrilled that at last I was part of a group of people that worked hard to save lives and was pleased to be able to do anything to help. I worked long hours, and didn't see much of my mother or family.

My mother was always very independent and well-organized. She made contact with her two sisters who still lived in Trnava and they met occasionally, secretly. Through them my mother met some other women who were still in Bratislava and were old friends and acquaintances. There were enough of them to start a bridge club, and so my mother played bridge again almost every afternoon. She was pleased about this; bridge was her special hobby and she was very good at it – in fact before the war she had been champion of Slovakia for several years running.

Thus the beginning of the summer was pleasant, and we felt quite secure. Josef kept me informed about the political and military situation and Aunt Manci managed to let us know that my father was in a work camp outside Budapest and was quite well. He was pleased that we were safe, and wrote to us through Manci describing his life in the camp. He was in charge of food supplies, so that at least he was not starving. Also some of his old friends were with him, and they were just waiting for the war to finish. The work they had to do was not too hard either. Yet, I was deeply concerned about my father, for I knew how much he must be suffering and how deeply unhappy he must be that he was unable to look after us and protect us.

Our feeling of relative security was rocked first by an accident my grandma had: she fell and broke her hip and we had to find a hospital where they would accept her for treatment and nursing. When finally we found an acceptable place, it was with great sadness that we took her there. As always, Grandma was the one who kept not only her own but also our spirits high. She was optimistic, and was concerned only about our safety, telling us not to come to visit her too often, in case we were recognized, followed and detained. Yet I knew how much she longed for our company in her lonely hospital bed and I went to visit her quite often, even though I knew it was taking a risk. Despite being in hospital, Grandma was strong and full of optimism and hope. This was easy during those early summer weeks, when the fortunes of the war had finally changed and the German defeat seemed so close.

MEETING WALTER

The news brought by Walter, my childhood sweetheart, who had been deported long ago, shattered my fragile peace of mind. When I next met Josef to hand over some work I had done for him in the office (a bunch of completed forms of various forged documents), he said to me quite casually: 'I've just met Walter. He's just returned from the concentration camp and is here in Bratislava. Would you like to see him?' Joseph might have guessed how I felt about Walter, and after I heard the news I was over the moon at the thought of seeing him. I eagerly agreed to meet him as soon as possible.

84

We arranged to meet the following afternoon. Joseph would come with Walter to a quiet place by the Danube and I would join them after I had finished work. Josef, considerate as always, tried to protect me and cautioned: 'Walter has had some very bad experiences, so he has changed a lot. He's not the same innocent child you remember.' I brushed the remark aside and said: 'Well isn't that true of all of us? We've all changed.' Little did I know that Walter's experiences were beyond anyone's imagination. Josef suggested that we meet on a little pebble beach on the banks of the Danube, where we often went swimming. We knew the place was very peaceful and we could talk there. The excitement and pleasure I felt at the prospect of seeing Walter must have shown in my face, for again Josef warned me: 'Please, be prepared to meet another man, not the one you know.' Somehow, these remarks that were meant to prepare me only increased my curiosity and anticipation at meeting my old friend.

The evening and next day seemed to drag on indefinitely. My mother noticed that I was unusually tense and that my thoughts were somewhere far away, where she could not follow them. She didn't even try to question me and after we had eaten she went out to see her friend. I spent a restless night, imagining a passionate reunion with Walter. I imagined that he would take me into his arms, kiss me full on the mouth and declare his eternal love for me. I was beside myself with joy and happiness.

At work I was unable to concentrate on anything and kept making mistakes in my typing, until finally shortly after lunch I said to my boss that I had a bad headache and asked him to allow me to have the rest of the day off. He smiled at me and said: 'I noticed there was something on your mind. Maybe it gave you a headache. Yes, I think you had better take the rest of the day off.' My boss seemed to know me better than I thought. So I took my bag with my swimming costume and towel and walked towards our meeting place by the Danube.

It was a warm sunny day and the pebbles by the bank of the river glistened like precious stones. I liked to collect them and bring them home, only to be disappointed when, away from the water they looked dull and uninteresting. I had about two hours left to daydream and watch the river flow by.

Josef and Walter were on time and appeared exactly as arranged. I jumped up to welcome them, Josef as usual smiling and good humoured, but Walter? Was this the boy I remembered and had loved just two years ago? I couldn't believe that a person could change so much in two years, even taking into account that an adolescent boy had passed into manhood. He had put on weight and although short, had a strong body and square shoulders. But it was his eyes that were so frighteningly different. Instead of the mischievous expression that I remembered, Walter's eyes were now staring at me with sadness and suspicion. Yet he was still my witty and intelligent friend, Walter; in spite of all these changes he was of course the same person and occasionally the old smile broke through. The wonder of seeing each other alive and of holding hands again overwhelmed me and I knew then that I truly loved him, perhaps for ever.

I realized that something terrible must have happened to him and even before we sat down I asked: 'Walter what happened to you during the last two years?' 'Let's sit down first,' Josef suggested.

The three of us sat down in that peaceful, idyllic spot, on a stretch of green grass by the river, and Walter began to tell us his story: 'Gerti, I was in a concentration camp where most of our friends from Trnava were sent to. They are all dead, apart from Freddie. Ernest, you remember, was your cousin Klari's boyfriend. He only survived one week, then he killed himself touching the electric wire fence that surrounded the camp.' At that point I interrupted him; I couldn't take any more and wanted to hear some more encouraging news: 'Walter, how did you manage to get out of there?' Josef, lying beside us on the grass, smiled, and suggested that perhaps Walter and I met on our own so he could tell me the story in detail; Josef had heard it several times already, and didn't want to hear it again.

For the rest of the afternoon we discussed ordinary things concerning our survival in Bratislava, such as how many of us had jobs to provide some money to run the workshop that produced forged papers, who had brought blank forms needed for birth certificates, and how long could the relative quiet last in Slovakia. Before parting, Walter and I agreed to meet the next day. A little further along the river, there was a small pebbly beach where the water was pale green and the current not too strong and it was there that we agreed to meet.

Next day was also hot and sunny; the sky was blue and cloudless – perfect weather for a relaxing day by the Danube! When I reached our meeting place, I settled in the shade of the large weeping willow. I knew that Walter would be late, he always was, and even when we were 12 I had always had to wait for him. I changed into my swimming costume and stretched out on the towel. It was so peaceful, with the sound of the moving river adding to the feeling of timelessness. In this idyllic spot on the banks of the Danube, it was hard to imagine that we were surrounded by war and killing, that as Jews, we were condemned one way or another to almost certain death. Perhaps it was the awareness of this that made the moment of peace so very precious. If only time could stand still and life could be like a gramophone record, where one could select the precious happy times and play them again and again, and delete those that were cruel beyond comprehension. These thoughts seemed foolish, but I was only 17 and in love, so perhaps I can be forgiven. While day dreaming about these unreal possibilities, I heard footsteps approaching.

I shook off my dreams, stood up and watched Walter walking down the steep narrow path towards our special secluded beach, carrying a bag and a briefcase. He waved to me and I was glad to see him smile. Yet when he came close I saw that his eyes took no part in the smile and the sadness – almost despair – stayed there in spite of it. There was a tense-ness and distance between us. I tried to disregard this and put my arms around him, but his body stiffened and I knew that my affectionate gesture was not welcome. So I suggested a swim. Maybe doing something ordinary, like going for a swim, and being carried by the current and then swimming against it and fighting it on the way back might help Walter to relax, and help us to bridge the barrier between us.

When Walter took off his shirt and shorts to change into his swimming trunks, I saw five numbers tattooed on his forearm. They were 44070, and I will never forget the horror I felt at seeing them, though I didn't know at the time what they represented. Walter noticed my expression and looked at me. A cool, cynical and almost cruel smile formed on his lips, but again the eyes did not change their expression. Sarcastically, he said: 'What are you staring at? This is my identity. For two years I had no name, I was just 44070. Where do you think I spent those two years? Do you think I was away, in a sanatorium, in a luxury recreation home?' I saw him fight the hatred that welled up in him at recollecting those two years and the hatred seemed now to be directed towards me. It was a feeling so deep, rooted in so much suffering that I was frightened of him. I didn't dare move and sat quietly waiting for him to regain his composure and perhaps explain what had driven him into this state. After a while, when we both sat silent and embarrassed, Walter gently put his arm around my shoulders and drew me close. I rested my head on his chest and waited, still apprehensive of his next reaction. He apologized quietly for being so aggressive, and said I would understand once he had told me exactly what was happening and what he had experienced.

He then described the elaborate death factory that had been built by the Germans in Auschwitz to destroy human life on an unprecedented scale. With remarkable, almost clinical, precision and self-control he described how this 'death factory' worked.

He told me not only the methods used, but also the capacity of the death factory – the sheer numbers of people that could be destroyed (liquidated) in the gas chambers in

Auschwitz – about the disposal of the corpses in the crematoria, and the sorting process of the possessions and other
remnants of the deportees that were killed in a place they
called 'Canada'. He told me that he had worked there for a
while and that it was quite a pleasant job, compared with
others. He described the arrival of the victims at the camp, the
opening of the doors of the cattle trucks, the horrible condition of the people on arrival. (Up to eighty people were
squeezed into one truck, old and young alike. During their
journey, which lasted up to ten days, they were given no
water or food and there was no sanitation.) When the doors
of the trucks opened they thought their ordeal was over, yet
as soon as they left the trucks the selection took place of those
that were to be gassed immediately and those that were to
survive for a short time to help to run the death factory. I
couldn't quite follow the details, it was all so extraordinary –
more like a nightmare than something that was really
happening. It seemed impossible that human beings could
devise such an evil system to destroy other human beings,
and find people to run it.

Walter described the methods used by the Germans to
break people's dignity and to make them accomplices to their
evil works, and how they almost invariably achieved the
human degradation of decent people. Yet in some, the human
spirit could not be broken and there was compassion, heroism
and courage to be found in many of the inmates. It was this
defiance to being dehumanized and brutalized by the system
that kept some of them alive. It finally helped Walter and his
friend Freddie to escape and tell the world the truth about
Auschwitz, in the hope that this information might stop the
slaughter.

Walter noticed that I was incredulous, and understood my
reluctance to accept his narrative. He said that most people
found it difficult to believe this terrible account, but that it was
true. He then said that the camp authorities were preparing to
increase their killing capacity so that they could liquidate the
Hungarian Jews who were due to arrive soon. He explained

that he would like to stop this, but in order to do so he had to get the truth about Auschwitz to the Hungarian Jews and to the attention of the allied governments. He was hoping that destroying the railway connection between Auschwitz and Hungary might delay the destruction of the Hungarian Jews. In fact the main reason for his escape was to inform the world of the German death factories, and to prevent the slaughter of the Hungarian Jews.

Walter also explained to me the extraordinary story of his escape. Auschwitz–Birkenau was 'protected' by an electric fence and surrounded by a system of watch towers, which were manned usually during the day. Under special circumstances, for example when someone had escaped, they were manned both day and night. Between the electric fence and the watch towers, there was a special area where prisoners were taken every day to work, and at the time of Walter's escape they were building 'facilities' for the expected Hungarian Jews. On return to the main camp, they had to confirm their presence, and in the evening they had a daily roll call. When someone was missing, an alarm was sounded and the area between the watch towers and the electric fence was searched. A close friend of Walter, who was caught trying to escape and was subsequently executed, told Walter before he died that he and his friend had constructed a hiding place within the working area between the electric fence and the watch towers. Two people could hide there for some time, and leave when the alarm was called off and the watch towers no longer manned.

The problem was that they had to have enough food to survive, civilian clothes and above all protection from being discovered by the Nazis and their sniffing dogs. So over a period of several weeks, Walter and his friend Fredi assembled food and clothes and hid them in the 'bunker'. To avoid being detected by the dogs, they prepared tobacco soaked in petrol and scattered it around the hiding place to stop the dogs from finding them. (Dogs do not seem to like the smell of tobacco and petrol. Russian prisoners of war who were brought to Auschwitz had given them this information.)

Walter and Fredi memorized the map and the roads leading from Auschwitz to Slovakia. When all was ready, they hid in their prepared hiding place and hoped for the best. They heard the sirens announcing the alarm and then the footsteps of the SS and the barking of the dogs. But their precautions seemed to work, and they remained undetected. Then, three days later, when the Germans had satisfied themselves that the prisoners could not be in the area between the electric fence and the watch towers, and must have got out somehow, the alarm was called off. Walter and Fredi crawled out and started their walk across Poland to Slovakia. To avoid detection by German soldiers or Polish collaborators, they walked only at night, avoiding marked roads, and headed south. They had run out of food and had no money to buy any. Approaching the Slovak border, they were helped by a Polish partisan and his mother to cross the border to Slovakia.

There, near a village called Skalice, they collapsed of exhaustion in a field and were discovered and nursed to life by a Slovak peasant.

When they recovered, they contacted the local Jewish Council, first in Čadca then in Žilina, who were none too helpful, and were reluctant to accept their story. They were sent to Bratislava to be interviewed by other more senior members of the Jewish Council and finally asked to write down their story and the information they had. They managed to compile a remarkably accurate account of the extent of genocide committed in Auschwitz by the Nazis.

Walter carried parts of his handwritten report in his brief-case and he gave me these notes to be typed during our frequent meetings that summer. When he handed me the last part of his report, he told me that it needed to be typed urgently. Somehow, with the help of friends, a meeting had been arranged between the papal nuncio and the two escapees from Auschwitz, namely himself and Fredi Wetzler. The meeting took place and the report was handed to the papal nuncio. Walter told me later that the papal nuncio was moved to tears on hearing their story and promised to do all he could to help. The report was also smuggled out to the Jews in Hungary and eventually reached England.

We were sitting under the willow tree; the sky was still blue and the sun hot. The water in the river rushed by as before and the place appeared to be the same as one hour ago when I had first arrived. Yet after hearing all this, I couldn't understand why a dark cloud hadn't appeared to cover the sun and the water in the river hadn't turned black. Outwardly nothing had changed, yet I knew that from now on, nothing would ever be the same again. This knowledge of the truth was a terrible burden.

Neither of us could think of swimming, or even staying in this peaceful place, so we dressed and returned to the dusty city. We walked quietly, holding hands. I felt betrayed by the world. Before we said goodbye, we arranged to meet again.

During the rest of that summer Walter and I met frequently but Walter was very secretive about his activities. He also asked me not to tell anyone that I was seeing him. Thus I never talked to my mother or her friends about it.

Walter could not stop himself talking about his experiences in Auschwitz and of the fortuitous events that helped him to stay alive, which he later described in his book *I Will Never Forgive*.

Perhaps that summer Walter and I became as close as we would ever get, though the distance and barrier between us never disappeared. The friendship and trust we had shared before these fateful two years, which I so hoped might return, was never recaptured. Somewhere in Auschwitz, Walter had lost the capacity to trust anyone.

In September, when the Russian army penetrated deeper into eastern Slovakia, there was an uprising of Slovak partisans, and some hope that for us the war would be finished. But this was not to be: the German army, with all its heavy artillery, crossed into Slovakia across the bridge that connected Bratislava to Austria without any difficulty or opposition, and occupied the country, giving full support to the Slovak fascist government and its fascist president Monsignor Tiso.

Walter, happy to be given the chance to fight the Germans, joined the partisans and left Bratislava to fight the Germans.

I felt lonely and vulnerable. I could not bring myself to share the knowledge of the horrors of Auschwitz with my mother or anyone else. The only person I could share my feelings with was Josef.

BRATISLAVA: SEPTEMBER–NOVEMBER 1944

During September–November 1944, my friends, Josef and his brother stayed on, but went into hiding, because rumour had it that the Germans were determined to cleanse Slovakia of the few remaining Jews. A detention camp was set up in a small town, Sered, and from there the Jews were sent to Auschwitz, Raabensbrück, Buchenwald and other destinations.

My Aunt Olga, and most of my family who were still in Slovakia, were rounded up and sent to Auschwitz. My mother's two sisters and their husbands that were in Trnava went into hiding and we had no contact with them.

My grandma, mother and I were now the only members of the family in Slovakia who had not been rounded up or gone into hiding. My grandma was still in hospital with her broken hip. She was registered under her own name and known to be Jewish. She and all those visiting her were therefore at risk. In spite of that I continued to visit her quite frequently, and it was perhaps after one of my visits that someone spotted me and followed me to our flat. In all likelihood, it was my aunt's maid who then denounced us, because not long afterwards the Gestapo picked us up.

7 One Week at the Gestapo, November 1944

THE APPLE

The small room we were taken to at the Gestapo headquarters in Bratislava had no furniture. There were no windows and the room had a padded door so that it was impossible to knock. The naked bulb that hung from the ceiling provided too little light for us to see the other people in the room clearly. Instead they seemed like shadows on the empty wall. The place was designed to isolate us all from the outside world, and to instil a feeling of complete isolation. As my eyes adapted to the darkness, I could see that, apart from me and my mother, there were four other people in the room, who had probably also been picked up during the night. I could feel the fear in that room: we were all frightened, for we knew that being interrogated by the Gestapo was not only going to be painful, but could also pave the way to the concentration camp.

I was standing quietly in the corner in my black leather coat, trying to assess the situation. My mother and I had been the last two people brought into this room, about an hour before, which would have been 2 o'clock in the morning.

Our capture was quite unexpected. We could not understand how we had been discovered, since our papers were excellent forgeries and could not be traced. Someone must have recognized us, followed us home and then denounced us. However it had come about, that night our sleep had been interrupted by a violent knock on the door, and shouts of 'Open up this is the Gestapo'. We knew immediately that this time there would be no escape, for apart from the front door there was no other access to our flat. Quickly my mother and I put on our dressing gowns and opened the door. In the doorway, two men dressed in black told us to get ready quickly, because we had to go to the Gestapo. We put on our clothes and coats; I put on the black leather coat that I loved to wear, thinking that I looked really tough and strong in it. On the way out of the flat, I grabbed two apples from the fruit bowl in the hall and put them in the pockets of my coat. Then we were ushered downstairs. The men kept on screaming at us: 'Move faster, you Jewish sluts, we haven't got all night just for you.' We were herded towards a black car. One of the men opened the door and shoved us into the back. After a brief ride we had arrived in this room.

I was aware that the Germans considered us Jews to be subhuman, and felt somehow that the fact that we were frightened would confirm these ideas in their minds. I was determined not only not to show my fear, but also to behave in an unexpected way, with confidence and arrogance.

My mother had already been taken to some other room to be interrogated. I heard the door open, and someone put his head into the room and shouted: 'The one in the leather coat.' I knew he meant me, for there was no one else wearing a leather coat. I moved slowly and deliberately, with apparent confidence – perhaps even arrogance – towards the door, keeping my hands in my pockets. The guard that came to fetch me had a pock-marked face and was very young. He reached out, trying to push me, but I was quick and moved past him through the open door into the brightly lit corridor, from where a door opened into the interrogation room. The guard pushed me in and forced me down onto a wooden chair facing my interrogator.

The bright light bulb that was directed straight into my eyes blinded me and made it difficult for me to see my inter-rogator clearly. I couldn't determine his military rank, and even had I seen it I wouldn't have known what it was, for I was never much interested in this kind of thing, I didn't even know what the different ranks were. Now I regretted it, for I felt it might have been useful to know. When my eyes adjusted to some extent to the bright light and I could make out my interrogator's appearance I saw a pale, pinched face. He was rather thin, and of uncertain age, somewhere between 40 and 50. He assumed that I could understand German, for as soon as I came in he started yelling at me in German: 'We know who you are, you filthy Jewish bitch', and then more abuse followed, obviously with the intention to frighten me. I was frightened even without the abuse, but I was determined not to show my fear. So I looked at my interrogator with outward calm, my hands still in my pockets. When the abuse stopped, I took an apple out of my coat pocket, directed my most charming smile at the interrogator and asked: 'Would you like an apple? I do have another one.' My interrogator, his face still angry, looked at me in utter amazement. His cold, cruel eyes examined me as he tried to assess the meaning of this bizarre behaviour.

Still smiling I said: 'It is a very nice apple, you know, and it would be good for you. You've had a long, busy, stressful night, and you need something to calm you down.' By now, the SS man was totally confused. Apparently this had never happened to him. After all, I was a prisoner, totally at his mercy. Usually people in this position were timid, frightened, in anticipation of the beating and torture we all knew was to be part of the interrogation. Most people acknowledged his power over them and behaved with appropriate reverence, or subdued resignation. Suddenly there was this young, arrogant, yet innocent-looking teenager, who seemed to have got it all wrong, offering him an apple and sympathy for his hard work, which consisted of torturing others. He wrinkled his forehead in confusion, rubbed his hands and stared at me coldly. I smiled back, friendly and relaxed, my hand still holding the apple. I started to enjoy the situation, as I became aware that he was utterly bewildered. He stood up from his chair, and he was much smaller than I had expected. He then proceeded to pace about the room, his hands behind his back and his chin held high. His blond hair was neatly combed, framing his pale face. His training told him that it was impossible for a Jew to behave like this. Jews were meant to be cowards, lousy subhuman frightened vermin. His puzzled expression betrayed his inner thoughts and confusion: 'Was there some mistake in this case?' His bewildered expression changed gradually into a friendly grin: 'You are probably right, I am tired tonight, and may make some mistakes. I will tell the guard to show you to your rooms.' He made it sound as though we were in some fancy hotel. We will talk again tomorrow. Good night.'

I got up very slowly, eating my apple: 'Thank you. Tomorrow you can ask me all the questions you want the answers to. We will both be less tired, and regrettably I am not in a position to disappear overnight.' With this and another radiant smile, I followed the guard who was escorting me to our sleeping quarters. The briefness of the interrogation, the fact that he had not been called in to beat me and that no violence had apparently been used during the interrogation confused the guard, who could not figure out why I had been treated in this strange way. In contrast to his previous behaviour, when he had tried to push me around, he was now quite courteous and polite, and showed me to the room where I was to spend the rest of the night.

FIRST NIGHT

The room was on the second floor of the building, and again, it had hardly any furniture. There were no beds or mattresses, just a large table in the middle. About thirty people were trying to find a spot to lie down on the bare wooden floor; some people were already lying on the table. There were men, women and children and surprisingly some families that were still together. All of them had been brought in only recently, a few hours or a day or two ago, so they looked quite well fed and clean, but most of them – even the children – had bruises on their faces and arms from recent beatings. In the silence that followed, with most of them asleep, I could still feel the fear. I shuddered, not because the cold damp October air filled the room, but because terror suddenly gripped me with such intensity that I couldn't control it. But I was amazed that by acting like an arrogant girl and behaving so differently from what had been expected I had taken my interrogator by surprise and he had spared me any rough treatment at least for the time being. I wasn't sure whether I would be able to continue this play-acting, and get my mother to do likewise. Only if both of us succeeded in convincing these men that we were indeed what our papers said, good Slovak citizens from the Eastern part of the country that was occupied by Russians and not Jews, did we stand a chance of getting out of here. But at that moment, on this cold October night, I had little hope that we would pull it off. And if we didn't, there was just one terrible train journey separating us from the hell known as Auschwitz.

The people in this room, this cold antechamber of death, were all ignorant of the extent of horrors and suffering in German concentration camps. What I knew about it from Walter's accounts weighed heavily on me and I was not sure how to handle it. Should I tell everyone what lay ahead of them? Would they believe me, and would it help them? As for myself I knew that I would never survive in a concentration camp; it would kill me just to witness the suffering and degradation. I couldn't see where my mother was, and wished I could be close to her and hold her in my arms and comfort her.

DAY ONE AT THE GESTAPO

As dawn was breaking, I tried to locate my mother. I was hoping that she was asleep, but when I saw her I realized what she must have been through. She sat in a corner, slim and frail, the grey coat wrapped round her body to keep her a little warmer, with her eyes closed and her face resigned. She looked so fragile, like a broken doll. Her lips were blue and bruised, and her left cheek swollen. So they have beaten her already, I thought, and we have only been here a few hours! How did she cope? What did she tell them? Probably not much, otherwise they would not have allowed her to meet me.

I knew that that morning most of the people in the room would be sent to Sered, where they would board the cattle trucks and be transported to concentration camps. Would my mother and I also join them or did we still have a chance?

I made my way towards her, careful to avoid waking the sleeping people around me. When I reached her I could hardly contain my sorrow and emotion. I gently put my arm around her shoulders and drew her to me. She woke up immediately and her brilliant blue eyes lit up at seeing me. She tried to smile, scanning my face to see whether I was unharmed. Bravely she said: 'It wasn't too bad, I only lost a tooth, and I didn't tell them anything. I stuck to the story we agreed on. They were quite rough at first, but then they mellowed, as though they doubted that they had the right people. It was quite strange – they almost apologised – I wonder what happened? And you Gerti, are you all right?' 'I am fine, no one laid a hand on me,' was all I managed to say. 'Mum, let's try to get some sleep now. Today will be a difficult day, and we have to get it right. We must get out of here, that is all that matters now, to get out of here together.' I couldn't explain why this was so important; anyway, not yet. My mother was very scared, and I was not sure how she would take the knowledge of what may be in store for us if we did not get out of there. For me this knowledge just now was both a burden and a source of strength and determination. As I looked at my mother, asleep once again, I recalled with unusual clarity my meetings with Walter and the account of the horrors of Auschwitz that he disclosed to me on that beautiful hot summer day in 1944 on the banks of the Danube, shortly after my mother and I had arrived in Bratislava from Budapest. I needed to recall all I had learned in order to help me to cope with the present and make the best of the disaster that had befallen us.

I was certain that I would never be able to protect my mother in a concentration camp, for Walter had told me how families were torn apart and not able to help each other. Rest and sleep were essential for both my mother and myself because the next day the game of having to impersonate the simple Slovak girl whose documents I had would continue and we would have to be alert. But nothing much happened on this first day, and we had an early night.

DAY TWO AT THE GESTAPO

The next morning, black water that was supposed to be coffee and a chunk of dark bread was handed out to everyone. Shortly the order was given for most people to prepare for departure. On the whole they were quite pleased to go; no more beatings and interrogations, and no one anticipated the horrors that awaited them. We were told that everyone was being taken to a work camp. Knowing that the war was nearing its end, most people believed that it would be possible to survive a few months of hardship in a work camp. No one even in their darkest nightmares could have imagined that the only work they might be involved in would be to assist the Germans in destroying and killing their fellow Jews. My mother and I and a few others were told that we were to stay behind because our position needed to be clarified.

With just a few prisoners left in the building, the Germans could focus their whole attention onto us. My day started by being taken unceremoniously to a small room in an ice-cold cellar, stripped to my underwear and locked in. There was very little room to move, but I managed to run on the spot and move as much as possible so as to avoid feeling cold. I did not know how long I was in the cellar, because my watch was taken away, but after what seemed to be a very long time another interrogator came to ask questions. He was tall, blond and exceptionally handsome in a Nordic way. Until he looked at me with an icy stare I thought he was truly wonderful. He took me by the arm. 'I will show you what will happen to you if you do not tell us the truth,' he said quietly. Then he led me out of my cell and opened the door to the neighbouring cell, which was equally bare and cold. Curled up on the floor was the naked form of a man bruised from what must have been repeated beatings. He lay there motionless and unaware of his surroundings. I was shown several examples of such atrocities in different cells in the cellar. I had to exert all my self control to remain impassive. I didn't say a single word as I was walked in and out of these cells, but my revulsion was deep and my determination not to succumb to my captors increased even more.

Suddenly we heard the noise of the air-raid sirens, signalling an air raid on Bratislava. Bratislava had an oil refinery that allied aircrafts attempted to disable. Several air raids had taken place already, and many ordinary houses had been hit, with some civilian casualties. Shortly after the sirens, the noise of explosions reached us. I was delighted. Even if these explosions killed me, I would have been killed by friends, and many Germans would also have been destroyed. I willed the bombs to hit this very building. My interrogator responded to this attack in a most peculiar way. It was as though he suddenly realized that the fortunes of the Germans in this war had turned, and that the allies would soon win the war.

HANS SEIDLINGER'S STORY

My interrogator became friendly and subdued. He no longer asked questions, but started to talk about himself. Apparently he had spent a year in Auschwitz, where he took part in the usual activities carried out by German guards. Unaware that I already had information as to what was going on in that camp, he told me about the selections, gas chambers and crematoria and all the other horrible things that he had helped to carry out while in Auschwitz. I was not particularly surprised of course; the events he described matched everything I already knew from Walter's account. What did surprise me was that this man told me about it without displaying any remorse or shame. I asked him how he could participate in such atrocities, and what motivated people to do so. He replied: 'It gives me great pleasure to feel that I can decide whether someone will live or die. The power over other human beings and their lives is an exhilarating experience.'

By the time he finished his account and we concluded this part of the conversation the air raid was over, and my interrogator and I returned to my cold cell. However, it was difficult to return to the previous phase of the interrogation. My interrogator had obviously something else on his mind after the air raid. 'I know that you are Jewish,' he said to me, 'and if you cannot prove the contrary you and your mother too will end up in Auschwitz. But I could help you to escape from here and hide you until the end of the war, provided you gave me an alibi after the war, and testified that I was helping Jews in the camps. Of course you would have to stay close to me, and perhaps even marry me so I could be sure you wouldn't stop helping me. By the way, I have not introduced myself. My name is Hans Seidlinger, and I come from Tyrol.' I was profoundly shaken by this proposal and for a few seconds I was undecided. Then I remembered how Walter cautioned me never to trust an SS man and his promises. Many of the prisoners believed them, gave them some hidden, or even stolen possessions to help them to escape, but were always betrayed, caught and executed. So I looked at Hans and, regaining my self-control said firmly: 'But Hans, this will not be necessary. We will be able to prove that we are not Jewish and that our documents are genuine.' I think neither Hans nor I really believed this statement.

I was proved right to reject the offer of help. Years later, when the war was over and the fate of my friends and acquaintances from Slovakia was traced, I learned what happened to a girl from Trnava whom I knew well, who was a year older than I, the daughter of my mother's bridge

102

partner. She too was held prisoner by the Gestapo shortly after my mother and I had been there. She was promised help to escape by the same Gestapo officer provided she became his mistress. He kept her at the Gestapo for a while, but as the Russian army advanced and the Germans prepared to evacuate Bratislava she was murdered in the cellar of the Gestapo building, probably by the same man who had been promising to help me.

In spite of my youth and lack of experience, I was convinced from the very first time I met him at the Gestapo that he could not be trusted and that I should not accept his offer of help.

I returned to our sleeping quarters as it was getting dark. My mother seemed to have had an uneventful day, and was worried about me. She was relieved when she saw that I was not hurt. I was however exhausted, and not sure what to tell her about my day with Hans. So I thought it best to try and get some sleep. As I was nodding off, I felt a hand stroking my forehead, and it was not my mother's hand.

When I had returned to this room after my day with Hans it was already dark and I hadn't noticed the young man who was sleeping next to us. Now I felt his breath and his hand touching me. It was a good feeling. Neither of us said anything, but we curled up close to each other and both got some comfort from this closeness. Gradually sleep took over. I needed the rest so as to be able to play the role of an innocent Slovak girl and help us both to get out of this place.

DAY THREE AT THE GESTAPO

The Key

Soon after 'breakfast' I was taken to be interrogated again. Another man in uniform sat behind a desk, a folder in front of him. On top of the folder was a key. 'We found this key in your pocket, and it does not fit any of the locks in your flat. Where is this key from?' I had to think fast, I couldn't say that

I had found the key on the street and just kept it, I had to find some plausible reason for having it. In fact the key was from my aunt's flat. She had given it to me in case we needed anything, blankets for example, so we could go to the flat at anytime and get them. The flat was rented to a young Slovak lawyer, Anton, who seemed happy, nice-looking and gentle. Although he did not know who I was he was kind to me when we met at the flat. Now what should I say about the key? I could not admit the real reason for having the key, for that would have identified us as relatives of a Jewish person, my aunt, who was in hiding. So what plausible story could I invent? Anton was probably a true Arian, and perhaps I could claim that I was visiting him. I found him very attractive, and in my childish fantasies I had imagined myself as his girlfriend. It came quite easily then for me to say that this was the key to my boyfriend's flat. 'My mother,' I said, 'doesn't know anything about this and it is really my secret.' Once I had started on this story I couldn't stop, and when asked for the address of the flat I had to give the interrogator the true address, for they could have checked whether or not the key fitted the apartment's door. So I gave them Anton's address, and hoped for the best. I hardly knew the man, and had no idea what his response would be when asked about me. Would he be imaginative enough to guess my position? I hoped that when confronted with an officer from the Gestapo he just might understand what is going on. I was told that this was all for now and was taken back to the detention centre.

I was agitated and worried, for this could be the end; our true identity could be discovered. I sat in a corner, hunched up, unable to talk to my mother about what had happened. So the minutes dragged by. It was about 2 o'clock in the afternoon when I was summoned again. I was taken to the same barren room, and the same interrogator who had spoken to me in the morning was there. 'We have your Anton here, he confirmed that you are his girlfriend.' I could hardly believe my luck. Suddenly I felt confident; and said: 'Can I talk to him?' 'Yes, but only very briefly, remember we do not trust you. You could be just a Jewish whore, and fooled Anton by pretending to be someone else. But all right, you can see him, it will be interesting to watch how you behave with him.' After a short while Anton came into the room, and we embraced, for the first time ever. Anton was very sweet. 'Are you all right, Gerti', he asked, 'Do you need anything?' I was so overwhelmed with emotion, admiring the sensitivity of this man, who was almost a stranger, that I could hardly say anything. 'Anton, all this is a great mistake, and I will be out of here soon. I can't wait to be with you again.' Keeping up the pretence he replied: 'Yes, darling, I miss you too and hope that all this will soon be forgotten.' Then he took my hand, and gently kissed it. I didn't know then that I would never see him again, that I would never be able to thank him for this. After the war, he moved away from Bratislava and although I tried to locate him I failed to do so.

Back in the detention centre the room was almost empty. My mother was crouched in a corner, badly bruised. My elation and confidence shrunk and as I looked at my mother I felt that all was lost anyway, that I would never be able to get her out of there. 'Gerti, they beat me, told me they knew everything about us and that you already confessed and told them who we were. I didn't tell them anything though, I held out.' Then she whispered quietly to tell me what I already knew: 'Gerti, I want this to end, I can't hold out much longer – the humiliation, the beating, all the lies and deceptions. Why not just confess, be what we are, go with the others. You are strong, you will survive, the war is nearly over, and I don't care any more.'

Now I had to tell my mother that there was hope for us, and that if we stuck to our story we might be released, but if we were sent away we were almost certain to die. I described my meeting with Anton, and how he had confirmed my story that I was genuinely who I claimed I was. So a major hurdle, the problem of the key, had been overcome. I was still dazed by the outcome of my encounter with Anton, by this minor victory of trust and human dignity. Surely my mother would see that it was not all doom and gloom, that there was hope not only for us, but also for this world. How could we give up now, on the brink of the end of the war, when so many people had fought and died to defeat this evil? I tried hard to persuade my mother not to give up. I defended my point of view, that we had to struggle to get out of here and stay alive. I was too young to understand how tired my mother was, and imagine how she could come to feel that maybe it was time to give up and join the rest of our people. I realized that she had tried to hold out because of me, and only me, and that she felt a failure, because she could not protect me. It must have been very hard for her to be alone, without her husband, sisters and brothers. 'Mum, listen to me, we will get out of here, I promise, and we will survive, but please do not give up, and follow my advice. Maybe the roles have changed and I can protect you rather than the other way round. Please, mum, trust me.'

DAY FOUR AT THE GESTAPO

The start of this day was no different from the others. After breakfast, my mother and I were summoned to the Gestapo office. Of course we were frightened, and didn't know what to expect. But for some reason, this morning everyone was quite friendly to us. I felt that maybe yesterday's confrontation with Anton had helped, but I wasn't sure. When we entered the office, a uniformed man received us, and asked whether we could clean the offices and light the fires in the stoves. The offices were on the first floor of the building and had large windows facing the street. Being there gave me a sense of freedom. We were given different offices to clean, I think there were about five rooms to do. We were given dusters, brooms, dustpans and all the usual cleaning utensils. A uniformed man watched us as we worked. Although I had always hated cleaning, this time I enjoyed being given the chance to be in this bright room, so I worked very slowly. As I was dusting the desk I noticed a packet of neatly folded rubber objects that I had never seen before. A paper band tied them together, and I was curious to see what they were. I tried to undo the paper, but couldn't, so when I spotted a pair of small scissors I started to work on the wrapping. Suddenly the uniformed man noticed what I was doing and pounced at me screaming, 'Don't touch it.' I was bewildered, because it didn't look like a dangerous object, so I couldn't understand why he was so agitated. 'Haven't you ever seen these?' The soldier shouted. Guessing from the expression on my face that I hadn't, he started to laugh. 'These are condoms,' he said, 'they are used to stop girls getting pregnant when we sleep with them. If you make a hole with these scissors in the rubber, they will be no good any more.' My curiosity aroused, I really wanted to have a good look at one of these strange objects, but it was obvious that the man would not show me any of them. Still, he was well pleased that I had amused him.

My next task was to light the fire in the stove. I had always been hopeless at doing this, probably because I was too impatient and did not wait long enough for the fire to really burn before putting on the coal. I had the same problem here. The soldier thought that I was faking this inability to light the fire, but finally he lost patience with me and helped me. By this time we were quite friendly, almost conspirators. 'Do not tell anyone that I helped you to light the fire, we are not supposed to talk to you.' he said as I finished with the cleaning. My mother, who was much more efficient than I, and probably hadn't come across interesting objects such as condoms in the office she'd been given to clean, finished her job long before me, and was back in our prison on the second floor.

It was lunchtime, and we had the usual brew and a piece of bread to go with it. We were just finishing, when we heard the sound of lorries stop outside the building. Some new prisoners must have arrived. Who were they? The guards started to lead the first arrivals into the detention centre. They were a pitiful sight. Some of them were singing, some of them couldn't walk properly, some had contorted movements. They were distressed and many of them screamed and thrashed about, but most of them were just bewildered and confused. Someone told us then that they came from a mental hospital near a village called Pezinok, and that they had been patients in that institution. Suddenly alarm bells began to ring; my uncle Karol had a son Martin who was a patient in that place. If he was among the patients brought in now, and he recognized my mother and me, our game was over. So I watched carefully as these poor people were herded into the room. There were about fifty of them now, and there was hardly any room left in the 'centre', yet there was no sign of Martin. Then the final group was brought in, and I saw him. He was, like the others, bewildered, but there was a strange dignity about him that I had never noticed before. He was quiet and silent, did not speak to anyone and when he noticed my mother and me did not show any sign of recognition, though I imagined that I saw a small spark in his sad brown eyes. The arrival of these poor patients, and the knowledge that they would all be slaughtered filled me with such despair that I forgot to think about our predicament. These people stood no chance. Most of them were unaware of what was happening; yet there was such a terrible fear in the group that made the whole thing more gruesome. Martin sat huddled on the floor, silent and pensive. My mother wanted to go to him and comfort him, but I stopped her: 'Mum, we mustn't show that we know him. I am sure that as soon as they discover his name they will associate him with us anyway, and confront us. I know how you feel, but you cannot help him and it could cost us our lives.' We both felt another slice of our dignity, our humanity, slipping away. Maybe my mother was right and there was nothing else to do than admit who we were and be taken away to our death. But I could not give up, my wish to live was stronger than any other feeling, and my head triumphed over my heart.

About two hours later, Martin was escorted away by one of the guards and then my mother and I were taken to the interrogation room. We both knew that we would be confronted with Martin and asked whether we knew him. I wasn't sure how it would end, and it depended very much on Martin.

We entered the room; Martin was sitting on a chair, a bright bulb shining in his face. As we entered, the Gestapo interrogator, one I hadn't seen before, shouted at Martin: 'What is your name?' Quietly, Martin whispered: 'Martin.' 'No, not that one, your surname you idiot.' Martin smiled quietly. 'I am an idiot, I do not remember.' 'I will jolt your memory you stupid fool,' screamed the interrogator. 'It is Sidon, isn't it?' Martin looked up, 'If you say so, you know better, I am only an idiot.' The scene was heart-breaking, and I knew that Martin was play-acting and realized what it was about. Then the interrogator turned to us and asked us to stand right in front of Martin. The light was turned onto us, so that Martin could see us clearly. 'These two women, are they also called Sidon? Martin, you have to tell the truth, you mustn't lie.'

Martin looked at us for a long while, and I was certain that he recognized us. My feelings were a mixture of fear, compassion and sorrow. What would my poor cousin say? I could not imagine for a moment that he did not recognize us, and how would his damaged mind interpret all this? Martin looked at us in astonishment. His arms were moving about uncontrollably, as they often did when he was excited. 'I do not know these women, I do not know their names,' he said finally. I was relieved, but at the same time a terrible sadness flooded me, and I could see that my mother was near to tears. So Martin, my poor mentally sick cousin had not given us away. How much he understood of what was going on I will never know. Then the interrogator turned to me: 'Do you know him?' He asked pointing his finger at Martin. 'I saw him for the first time here when he was brought in. I've never seen him before.' And then he asked my mother: 'What about you?' 'I haven't seen this boy before, I don't know him.' I felt that my mother was near to collapse; she could not take any more. I only hoped that we would be out of here soon. Then to my surprise my mother lifted her head and asked: 'What will happen to him and the others that you brought in and need care?' There was surprise in the interrogator's face, for he was not used to being asked questions, that was his job. But he quickly recovered and said: 'That does not concern you. They will be taken care of.' And so they were: in the ovens of Auschwitz.

Back in the detention room, with all the patients from the psychiatric ward, the noise was almost unbearable. There was one person screaming, 'I am God, I will save the world,' while another was rocking from side to side, tearing at her hair and shouting: 'I do not want to die, send me home.' The scenario changed constantly as the fifty or so people crowded into a small space tried to settle. They were, after all, mentally disturbed people and were entitled to display behavioural disturbances, yet to me they seemed much more 'normal' than our jailors. They were not offensive or even abusive to each other and thus completely harmless. Why did they have to die, while so many others who were killers and dangerous psychopaths were left free and were supported in their activities?

My mother and I felt gloomy and apathetic. My mother's depression deepened as she watched Martin, and felt drawn to him. I think in some way she almost envied him that for him it was all solved, for tomorrow they would all go to a detention camp in Sered and from there to Auschwitz, while we would still be left here to continue our fight for survival.

DAY FIVE AT THE GESTAPO

The next morning, two lorries stopped outside the building and all the patients were loaded on to them. My mother and I were again taken to clean the Gestapo's offices. While I was cleaning, Hans Seidlinger came and announced that after lunch I would be taken to our flat with him and another guard, and the flat would be searched. I was surprised that they hadn't searched the flat before, but then maybe they had and there was some strange ploy in this planned outing with me. I was very worried, mainly because I did have some forged documents hidden in the flat and some stationery that was necessary for producing forgeries. Also, I was suspicious because I did not see any need for me to be present at the search, and I reckoned that Hans had some strange motive for taking me with him.

Yet again I was thrown into a panic. This search of our flat was very dangerous, but on top of that I couldn't understand why I was to be present. At around 2 o'clock a guard came to fetch me, told me to put my coat on and come with him. He took me to the gate and the black car that had brought us was waiting. Hans was in front in the passenger seat and another Gestapo officer was the driver. They had our address in a brown folder that probably contained other information about our case. It was raining outside and the grey sky mirrored my mood. I had the distinct feeling that this trip would dash our last hope of convincing the Gestapo that we were not Jewish and that our forged papers were real.

We arrived at the apartment block where our flat was and I was told to get out of the car and to lead the way to our flat on the first floor. I tried my best to look unconcerned and cheerful, as though there was nothing to worry about. Hans had the keys to the flat, but he gave them to me and ordered me to unlock the door and let us all in. Everything in the apartment looked exactly as we had left it. The sitting/dining room was tidy and ordered; the kitchen too was clean, only the bedroom showed signs of our hasty departure. The bunch of blank forms to be used for forged documents had been hidden between two panels of wood in a collapsible table in the sitting room. The flat looked as though it had not been searched, but I could not be sure, and it was possible that Hans already knew about the documents. I felt sad and nostalgic being in the place where my mother and I had spent the last few months, hoping to survive till the end of the war. Yet I continued to try hard to look unconcerned. 'I can't wait to be back here and out of that awful room where you keep us,' I told Hans. 'Well, Gerti,' he said, 'it really depends on you whether that will be possible.'

I didn't reply to this nonsense, for obviously our stay at the Gestapo was not voluntary. Hans sent the other man to search the kitchen, and I was to stay with him while he searched the sitting room and the bedrooms. There was nothing for me to do, so I sat down and waited. Hans was opening drawers, looking through books and papers. Then suddenly he looked under the table and saw that there was something there. Without much effort and further search he removed the papers and looked at me. 'What is this?' he asked pointing at the stack of about twenty empty forms to be used to forge birth certificates. There was nothing I could do and no point in denying that these documents belonged to me and that I had hidden them.

Hans was delighted with his find, for he now had control over me, and that was how he liked it. He dragged me into the bedroom, while the other German was searching the kitchen. In the bedroom Hans made it clear that I could avert disaster if I slept with him. He took me in his arms, quite gently, and whispered: 'I will look after you, darling, if you allow me to make love to you.' I felt horrified, and yet was not the value of our lives much greater than the humiliation of being subjected to some physical exercise, from which it might be possible to completely detach oneself? I had never been with a man, and never even felt that it was important, for in these matters I was very far behind others of my age. So I said: 'Look Hans, you know that I find you very attractive, but we can't do anything here, we're not alone.' He agreed and said that he would arrange something and find some place where we could be together. So with that arrangement in place we returned to the car with the rest of the crew and were driven back to the Gestapo at Edlová 6.

As soon as I entered the building I knew that something terrible had happened. All the rooms were full of sick, old people, moaning and crying. There was no attempt made to help any of them, and since most of them could not walk they had to relieve themselves wherever they happened to be. The stench was unbearable, and the scene even more so. I was immediately summoned to the interrogation room, and treated quite differently from any other time. First I was beaten up, then told that now they knew for certain who we were. My grandma Jeanette had been brought in with the others who were hiding in the local hospital and my mother had admitted that she was her mother-in-law. I knew that I had lost my battle and did not argue, but the interrogator wanted to get his own back on me for giving them so much trouble and not telling 'the truth'. Dazed, I was taken back into the detention room, where my mother found me. She cried, when she saw all my bruises, but I knew that no serious damage had been done. I saw Grandma, my sweet grandma, who was such an important person for me when I was a child and who had really brought me up. She was lying on the floor, because she had a broken hip and could neither stand nor sit. She looked at me and said: 'I had tried to claim that your mother was a stranger to me, that I had never met her and I kept repeating it to them. But your mother could not deny she knew me and burst into tears when she saw me. Then when they asked her whether I was her mother she said: no, my mother-in-law. After that they just took us away and dumped us here.'

I looked at my mother in amazement. We had been so close to being freed, and I had been prepared to subject myself to the ultimate humiliation to get out of this place and avoid being killed, yet my mother could not control her emotions! I was really upset with her, and yet wanted to hear her side. 'I know that I've done a terrible thing, and perhaps you can't understand me, but I just could not deny that I knew Grandma. Seeing her as she was there, in pain and agony, I could not say that she was a stranger. Maybe you will understand one day that sometimes even living is not worthwhile denying one's dignity. I do not regret what I have done, but I feel that I had no right to jeopardize your chances of living.' How very different, and much more human and dignified my mother's attitude was compared to mine. I was focused only on survival at almost any cost, while my mother kept her human dignity. I was ashamed and yet could still not quite accept the situation.

I tried to be kind and to pretend that I accepted this development, that it might after all be better to be together and to help each other, though I knew from Walter that this would be impossible and that we would soon be separated. I also knew that there was no hope of survival for Grandma and so my mother's sacrifice of our lives seemed futile. In my blinkered state I did not understand that even a few hours of comfort, and the dignity of being together enjoying the love and family ties we shared might be more important than life. Later, much later in life I not only understood my mother, but also appreciated her bravery and dignity.

That night nobody slept much, not only because of the moans and stench and the pitiful sight of the old and sick, but also because we all knew that tomorrow we would be taken away to Sered. This, I knew, was the time when I had to tell my mother about what to expect in the concentration camp. We were lying close to each other, and I hugged my mother, while I whispered to her what I had learnt from Walter. I told her everything I knew and spared her no details, and that may have been a mistake, but I felt I had to be honest with her, to encourage her to be determined to join me in our fight for survival. I told her that in the camp we would be separated. She would not be able to be either with Grandma or me, and Grandma would probably be killed on arrival, because she was sick, but we might last for a while. I also told her that I did not think that I could survive in a camp, and that the only way we could survive was to escape.

My mother listened to me, tears streaming down her face: 'Forgive me, Gerti, but I don't want to live in a world where things that you are telling me happen. I can't lose my dignity and exchange it for life. Please, don't force me to carry on with you, I can't. But I feel guilty that by confessing who we are to the Gestapo I betrayed you as well and that it may cost you your life. If you can escape and fight on your own, please do so, but I can't follow you. I have neither the strength, nor the will to live after what you have told me. Take this ring with you, and escape on your own.' She offered me her diamond ring, her engagement ring, but thinking it over, I decided that I could not part with her and would not try to escape. I told her so, and she didn't say anything. I held onto my mother, and admired her strength and courage. But still I wasn't sure of my feelings my wish to live was stronger than anything else.

DAY SIX AT THE GESTAPO

The morning started as usual with some sort of breakfast and then with me and my mother being escorted to the offices to do our daily cleaning job. The windows of the offices opened onto the street, next to the main gate, which was usually guarded. This particular November morning was the start of a typical autumn day: dull and hazy, and raining heavily. My mother and I were taken to two different offices. On the way, I told her that in spite of what I had said to her last night I was going to try and escape. I begged her to come with me. Not only was she not willing to do so, she was also worried about me in case I failed and got hurt in trying to escape. She no longer had the will to fight. I didn't argue, and as I cleaned, I gave up the idea of escape. I too was resigned to accept my fate.

But then the guard went away. I was shaking out the duster through an open window and noticed that the guards were not outside the gate as usual, probably because of the heavy rain. I went to my mother, who was sweeping the room, and told her that we shouldn't miss this opportunity and that I would help her to jump out of the window and then follow her. She refused to come near the window, whereas I couldn't keep away from it, looking out at the promise of freedom and life. Suddenly, the desire to live overcame me with such force that it eliminated all other considerations and I jumped out of the window. Once on the street I was surprised as well as shocked by my action. All my decent intentions to stay with my mother were suddenly broken, and now there was no way back.

I had to get away from this building as fast as possible. I knew the street quite well and remembered that one of the houses had a passage that had its exit in a street parallel to the Gestapo building. So I took the passage and then walked and walked fast, as far as I could. I was quite conspicuous, for I had no coat, only a blue, long-sleeved checked flannelette blouse and blue skirt. I couldn't even pretend that I was just trying to get quickly from one house to the other, because I was soaking wet. I had no money, and no one to turn to who I knew would help me. In spite of my terrible feeling of guilt, I was at the same time elated, for I was now free, and had succeeded at least for now in avoiding the destiny that had been planned for me by the Germans. To quell my feeling of guilt, I made up all sorts of foolish plans to get my mother out of Sered.

8 New Freedom, What Now?

It was still dark and raining as I hurried away from the building on Edlová 6. The pain I felt in knowing that my mother was still there almost quenched my joy at being free, breathing the cold air of this grey morning. Yet some very pressing decisions had to be taken immediately; I couldn't keep walking the streets, with my thin skirt and flannelette blouse getting wetter and wetter, without arousing suspicion, and a search for me was probably already underway. I couldn't stay on the street, and I needed shelter, help and money in that order. As for shelter, what where the options? I couldn't go to any of my friends or relatives who were in hiding. Although I was sure that I had not been followed, I couldn't risk this for it might endanger them and was not safe for me either. Still, I needed somewhere safe to stay for a few days until I could somehow obtain new forged papers, yet another identity, and money.

Once I had solved these problems I could perhaps decide what to do. I would have loved to have joined the partisans in the Slovak mountains, but had no idea where they were or how to reach them. I also knew that I was not very good 'fighting material', because I hated violence.

As I walked the streets, half dazed by the recent event of my escape, it was hard to get my brain to function. Gradually, the enormity of what I had done dawned on me, and I realized that my impulsive flight from the Gestapo, and leaving my mother, had changed my life forever and that I would always have to cope with the guilt of deserting her. It was true, she hadn't wanted to come with me, but then perhaps I too should have stayed. These thoughts and feelings of guilt made it very hard to think clearly and find solutions to my present problems.

To whom could I turn without exposing them to danger? Everyone who could help me would put themselves in danger and the penalty for helping a Jew was very severe indeed. It would have to be someone who would not be suspected, and therefore someone I hardly knew. Suddenly it occurred to me that Martin, my boss at work, appeared to be a very decent young man who didn't know me before I started to work there and might be prepared to help. Of course, I hadn't been to work for the past week, and he had no news of me, unless the Gestapo had contacted him and asked about me. But I didn't think they would have done, because I never told them that I had a job, and for some reason they were not interested. This was important, because it meant that no one would know that I had any connection with Martin. Thus, although Martin might have guessed that something was wrong, he had no idea what had happened. However, though he might not be suprised to hear the news, I couldn't begin to guess how he would react, and whether he would sympathize and take the risk of helping me.

The office opened at 8 o'clock and it was now only 7.30. Wandering the deserted streets, hungry, thirsty, cold and wet, I had at least one hour to wait. I was worried about staying out on the street, for wet and without a coat I was quite conspicuous. I had to find a place where it would be safe for me to wait. I remembered how, with my mother, having crossed the border from Slovakia to Hungary, we found shelter and protection in the small village church. Thus I began looking for a church in which to hide. I found one in the old town by Michalska brána (Michael's gate) and waited patiently inside. I was very cold and time went by slowly but eventually it was 8.30, time for me to make the phone call to Martin.

In the breast pocket of my blouse I had some loose change. I found a public phone box, lifted the receiver and dialled the number of the office. Fortunately, Martin answered the phone himself, so no one else in the office would know that I had called. I didn't tell him much, just that I was in trouble, and could he meet me. He wasn't even puzzled, or surprised, which made me think that he knew all along that I wasn't simply a young Slovak secretary. He too didn't talk much, just gave me the address of a small coffee house and told me to wait for him there. I knew the place, it was only a short distance from where I was phoning, and I walked there quickly. I still wasn't sure about Martin and his loyalties. All he had to do to protect himself was to phone the Gestapo or police and tell them where they could pick me up, but somehow I felt certain he wouldn't do this. Still, when I reached the coffee house I hid in the doorway of a house and waited to see whether Martin would come alone or with other people. Finally I saw him entering the coffee house alone. Still I waited for a while to see if he had been followed. When no one seemed to have done so, I went in.

Martin had chosen a table at the far end of the room, and was facing the door. It worried me a bit that I would be so far away from the exit, but perhaps it didn't matter. I must have looked a sight, with my wet hair, soaking wet blouse and skirt and no coat on this cold November morning, and I think my appearance prepared Martin to hear something rather unexpected. I sat down, and Martin ordered coffee and cakes for both of us. All the squares on the blue and white checked tablecloth were the same size, so there was some order in the world, and that calmed me a little. I concentrated on these squares to calm down enough to be able to explain coherently what had happened. Martin was composed and didn't seem nervous. He waited patiently for me to tell him what had happened, and why I had asked him to come and meet him. I didn't know where to start, but knew I had to tell him everything.

I started by telling him that I was not what I had pretended to be, and that I had deceived him. I told him that I was Jewish and had forged papers so that I could pretend to be a Slovak

119

girl. Then I wanted him to know that I had just escaped from the Gestapo and that any contact with me might be dangerous for him. This he had to know, so that even now he could tell me that he could not help me under these circumstances. But he took this information very calmly and asked me to tell him more about my family and myself. He made it clear that he was prepared to help me whatever my present circumstances, and in spite of the danger to himself. I told him in more detail how all the time I had worked for him I was deceiving him, that my real name was different from that he knew me under and that I was Jewish and trying to avoid deportation. I told him about my family in Trnava, my father who was still somewhere in Hungary and my mother whom I had so ruthlessly abandoned that morning at the Gestapo.

When he asked me finally, 'So what do you want to do now?' I tried to explain to him my tentative plan, which even at this stage was very vague: 'I would like to go to Hungary again, because Russian troops are advancing quite rapidly towards Budapest. Also I have family and friends in Budapest who could help, and I want to find my father. But to do that I need to get some money and new forged papers so that I can take a train to the Hungarian border. The most important thing is, I need time to make these arrangements.' And this I told him was where he came in. 'Could you give me shelter for about three weeks?' This was the main and very serious request I had to make and it was no small favour to ask. The few seconds he took to answer seemed like an eternity to me; so much depended on his answer, and I knew it was not an easy decision for him to make. I knew nothing about him – whether he had a wife, children or parents living with him and his answer may have depended entirely on these circumstances. As I watched him making up his mind I thought of completely irrelevant things, how handsome he was, how I admired his sense of humour and his vitality. When finally he turned to me and said: 'Yes I will help you,' I could hardly believe it. And then he told me what we would do. He suggested that I should stay that day and night in his apartment, which he shared with his wife. His wife would give me something sensible to wear. Then he suggested that the next day I should move to a friend's apartment. I agreed that this would be safer, because there was a slight chance the Gestapo might trace a connection between me and Martin, but were less likely to trace the friend who lived alone in a small apartment, and was quite frequently away. He was going to be away for a while in the next few weeks, and Martin thought that I could stay in his flat until I had got things sorted out and could go to Hungary. I was grateful that he didn't tell me to be careful, to watch out whether I was followed, and not lead anyone to his or his friend's house by accident. It showed that he had confidence in me being sensible. He paid the bill, gave me some money and an address on a piece of paper. 'My wife is at home today, and it is better if you go to this address alone by tram number eleven and then enter the building inconspicuously and go to my apartment. I will phone my wife and she will expect you. You can have a rest, dry your hair and clothes and wait for me. Don't start making arrangements yet; wait until I come back from work. I will hurry back and make sure that nobody has noticed anything unusual in the office. Now you had better be on your way.'

I did as I was told. The apartment was on the outskirts of Bratislava and it took me about thirty minutes to get there. Martin's wife opened the door. She was young, pretty and cheerful, told me she was called Natalia, and sent me off to the bathroom with a wonderful thick towel. She also supplied me with a dry skirt and blouse. It was a real luxury to have a hot bath, the first since I had been taken to the Gestapo. She also gave me a toothbrush. When I had finished in the bathroom I felt like a new person. I dressed and then explained to Natalia everything that had happened. I was surprised that she was quite casual about it all, not at all flustered or worried; in fact she behaved as though there was nothing strange about a Jewish refugee/escapee from the Gestapo landing on her doorstep. She treated me like a friend who just happened to need a bed for a while. This attitude

121

had a calming influence on me and I, too, almost believed that my being in this place with total strangers was the most natural thing in the world. And yet, she didn't tell me anything about herself, and I never found out what she really thought and to what extent her attitude was inspired only by her loyalty to her husband. However, I did feel that she liked me and was appalled by the terrible treatment of the Slovak Jews.

When Martin came home we had dinner. He told me that he would take me to his friend's apartment the next morning, and that I could sleep on their sofa just for one night.

8 NOVEMBER

First thing in the morning, Martin took me to his friend's apartment, which was only a short walk away and put me up in a little cosy box room. I was told that I could use the kitchen and cook whatever I wanted from ingredients that I could find in the cupboards. Juraj, Martin's friend, was hardly ever home, so I was given the keys to the flat, where I was to be mostly on my own.

Immediately after Martin left, I started to make my plans. I wanted to get away from Bratislava as soon as possible, for I was scared to go anywhere in case I met someone who would denounce me, or worse, some of the guards from the Gestapo who might recognize me. But to make my arrangements I had to go out.

So I walked the streets in Natalia's warm navy winter coat, with a large scarf wrapped around my neck that partly concealed my face. The first thing I needed was money. Someone in Trnava who knew my parents and knew where they had left their valuables might help. The most likely person was Mr Pavelka, my father's friend from Trnava. To find his phone number I had to go to the post office and look up phone numbers in Trnava. I found the number quickly and phoned him. To my surprise he was pleased to hear from me, and immediately offered to help. He asked how much money I needed. I told him the amount of money I thought I would need and he said that he could afford to give me the money. We arranged to meet in Bratislava outside the post office the next day. I couldn't believe my luck, and was deeply moved. My father's trust in Pavelka was justified, and it was also a reflection of the respect my father commanded, because it was because of his relationship with Pavelka that I was being helped.

The next task was to reach my friends who were still at large and who worked hard to help other fugitives like me by providing forged papers. I phoned Josef, who had helped me before. The phone was answered by a female voice, which informed me that Josef had left and was no longer working there. This news alarmed me, for it meant almost certainly that he had either been caught or was in hiding. My other contact was Jan, a friend from Trnava, who was in Bratislava and might know someone who could help me. I did not have his telephone number or address so I went to the house of friends of his family, who might know where to find him. They knew Jan's address and gave it to me and I started out to visit him straight away. All the time, I watched to see whether I was being followed and made sure that I was safe before I reached the house where Jan lived. When I arrived at the house, on the outskirts of Bratislava, I pushed a message for Jan through the door, asking him to meet me the next day in town. This was all I could do on this first day after my escape.

I felt exhausted and very worried about my mother. I had all sorts of plans, quite unrealistic ones, about how to get her out from the camp in Sered, where she had probably already been taken ready for deportation to a proper concentration camp. I thought that I could get forged papers for her and smuggle them into the detention camp and then give her instructions on what to do; or else I imagined that I could just bribe the guards and get their help to let her out. I was so obsessed by these fantasies that I almost believed this miracle would happen and that I would somehow manage to arrange her escape. These plans and fantasies helped me to worry less about my own situation and future. They also helped to ease the gnawing feeling of guilt associated with my escape.

But, by the time I finally got back to Juraj's flat, had eaten and gone to bed, I realized with despair that there was no way that I could help my mother, and that she wouldn't accept help anyway, whatever happened. I wondered how she was and whether she was still with Grandma. Poor, brave Grandma; she knew that she would die, and was resigned to it. She would have wanted me to escape, and I drew strength from this knowledge. If only I could tell her that I was OK, she would feel so much better. As for my mother, the war was so close to the end that I thought maybe I would see her again, provided she decided that she wanted to live. Without me there to help her to make this decision it was unlikely that she would survive. What a terrible burden of responsibility to carry at the age of 17.

9 NOVEMBER

My meeting with Mr Pavelka was at midday. I went to the post office a while before he was due to arrive, just to observe the scene. He arrived exactly as arranged. We shook hands and talked as we walked. He asked after my parents, particularly my father, and told me that our shop and house in Trnava had been taken over by our former shop assistant, Mr Simončič, and that it was doing very badly. Mr Simončič was drunk most of the time and did hardly any work. I felt almost ashamed that I had no interest whatsoever in this; I couldn't have cared less if I'd heard that all of Trnava had collapsed into a heap of rubble. Somehow things like shops and buildings seemed irrelevant. But I listened patiently to the news. When we had run out of things to talk about, Mr Pavelka took out a big wad of money. He told me that he had got me 30,000 crowns (about £500), and that he hoped it would help. It was a lot of money and I was deeply moved by his generosity. This was more then enough to help me to get forged papers, travel permits and any help I needed. It also meant that I could give some money to my host for putting me up. Mr Pavelka was a little embarrassed, and told me that he hoped to see my family and me soon, because the war was nearly finished. He also assured me that all the things we had left in his care (silver and my mother's jewellery, for example) were safe. Then he embraced me and left.

I had to wait another hour for the meeting with Jan and I walked the streets to pass the time. I kept a close lookout to see whether or not I was followed, but I was now quite well disguised and inconspicuous, so I was not too worried. As I walked around, I happened to pass the house where my mother's sister Jety and her daughter Lilly where hiding. Suddenly, I felt danger. I hid in the doorway of a house and spotted the black car used by the Gestapo just outside the house where my aunt Jetti was staying. Two women were being herded into the black car. I was agitated and very frightened and stayed hidden in the doorway until the time came for my meeting with Jan. I was so scared that I was imagining Gestapo officers and policemen everywhere.

Again, I came to the meeting place a little while before the arranged time to check out the situation. Everything seemed fine, and the coast appeared to be clear. To my delight I saw Jan, but I waited to make sure he was not being followed. Only when I was absolutely sure that he was alone did I approach him. He looked well, but worried. He seemed to be pleased to see me, and obviously had no idea that I had been caught by the Gestapo and escaped. I told him my story and then asked: 'What happened to Josef?' Jan then explained that Josef had had to go into hiding because he had been denounced, but had managed to escape before the Gestapo got to him. I was glad that Josef had escaped, but worried that without him I might not be able to get forged papers. Jan guessed what I was thinking and said: 'You remember Josef's younger brother Dov, the boy with a limp?' When I nodded in agreement he continued:

125

'Dov is now running the operation from a well-hidden basement office that is equipped with machines and craftsmen to produce the most sophisticated forgeries. I will send him a message that you need help, but it will take a while for the message to reach him. You will have to wait a day or two.' We agreed that I should come each day at different times to a different meeting place and wait for Dov or some other person to come and make the arrangements. We also agreed on a password to use. Jan informed me that the round up of the remaining Slovak Jews was now in full swing and that it was difficult to keep out of the Gestapo's clutches. All the Jews who had had special permits to stay because of their importance to the economy had now been taken and sent to camps. Only those in hiding remained, and many of those had been denounced and taken away. Thus the situation was very bad. Jan then said that he too was worried and hardly went out, so we hastily said goodbye to each other and went our own way.

The waiting was awful, and I had three days of it. My only job during the next three days was to turn up at the pre-arranged meeting place, hang around, and then with aching heart and terrible disappointment return to my hideout.

To make the time pass more quickly I kept cleaning the flat, washing the windows, polishing the furniture and the parquet floor. Unfortunately these tasks did not occupy my mind, which lingered on memories of all the people I had lost and those that were still in danger. The hours dragged on, and it seemed to me that each day lasted for months.

Some evenings, Martin or Natalia came to bring me some food and to chat for a while, and these times were the most precious part of the days that I spent in the flat.

13 NOVEMBER

Finally after four endless days on 13 November a young woman appeared at the place where Jan and I had arranged to meet. She was blonde and pretty, and as soon as she saw me, she approached me and said the password. Relieved I replied with the agreed reply. Then she said: 'I am Anna, Dov's friend, and I have to take you to him to start preparing your papers.' We went together to the outskirts of Bratislava, where Dov had his workshop in the basement of an old dilapidated farmhouse. She took me in and Dov gave me a hug and asked what it was I needed and what my plans were. 'I want to go to Budapest,' I told him, 'my father is still there and the Russians are closing in on the city, so I might be able to survive there.' 'So you will need identity papers and a travel document to get to the border,' Dov said. 'When do you want to go?' 'As soon as possible,' I replied. Then I asked what he thought about my plans to get my mother out of Sered when I had got my travel documents. He looked at me in an odd way and then said: 'I don't think you know what is going on here. The Germans have decided to get rid of all Slovak Jews as quickly as possible – your mother won't be in Sered any more, because transports are leaving every second day. Your plan was difficult enough anyway, but it's no longer possible to do anything.' Then he looked at me and added: 'Gerti, the war is nearly over, in a few weeks all the camps will be freed. Your mother is strong, she will survive. You have to think about your own fate, and also whether you can help others. If you are going to Hungary I will give you some contacts for people who could use your help.' The possibility of doing something useful brought back my resolve and my will to fight.

The formalities of my papers were then discussed. I needed a photograph, I had to choose a name and identity. All this took a while. 'How long will it take for my papers to be ready?' I asked, and to my disappointment the answer was: 'About ten to fourteen days. If we want to do a good job it will take us that long. There are so few of us and we are scattered all over the place, so it takes a long time. Could you meet Anna in ten days' time at the same place and same time as today? Hopefully she will have all you need.' I wanted to give him money for his expenses, but he was quite offended and refused. I also asked him whether he could get some Hungarian currency for me, or at least enough to buy a train ticket from the border to Budapest. He promised to get me some Hungarian currency. I asked after Josef and Dov said that he was OK, 'We managed to rescue him before the Gestapo came for him and he has a safe hiding place. I will tell him that you are alive, and well. He is very fond of you. Goodbye, for now, and good luck. I won't see you before you leave. You are a brave girl. I am proud of you,' he added in a fatherly voice.

Back in the flat, the days dragged on and on. There was no more cleaning and polishing to do and instead I tried to write a diary, some poetry, and notes about the present situation, but it was hard to concentrate. I also read some books I had found in the house, though I had little idea what I was reading. All I could really do to reduce the tension was bite my nails.

Finally the date of my appointment came around and it was time for me to go to the rendezvous. I arrived at the appropriate place full of excitement that my papers would be ready. I waited a long time, but no one came, and I realized that my papers were not ready. So back I went and somehow survived the next twenty-four hours. As I set out the next day I had almost lost hope of ever getting the papers. But then I saw Anna waiting for me. I could barely bring myself to follow the usual precautions and prowl around to see whether we were alone, I was so eager to get my documents. Since we had met before we did not need to use a password and when Anna saw me she came over to greet me, smiling. 'It's all ready for you, Gerti,' she said and handed me the briefcase she carried. 'The papers are there and a list of contacts in Budapest, members of Dov's Zionist organization that he would like you to get in touch with so you can give them a hand if they need you. Please memorize the names and destroy the list.' We both felt that we should quickly separate and not hang around with the documents and so we said goodbye, wished each other good luck, and went our separate ways.

I never knew what happened to Anna. I had no idea even then whether she was Jewish or a nice, very brave Slovak girl. I hope things turned out well for her, whoever she was.

As soon as I reached the flat, I took out the papers, checked everything, learned my new identity and prepared to leave the next day. I memorized the names of my contacts in Budapest, tore up the list and flushed the pieces of paper down the toilet. Juraj was away so I couldn't tell him that I was leaving, so I went to my ex-boss's flat to thank him. His wife packed a little suitcase for me with the most essential things, such as a change of underwear, a new blouse and skirt and other small items. Then they both embraced me and stopped me from saying thank you. 'It is us who are lucky that you gave us a chance to help you,' Natalia said. I was holding back my tears, and promised myself to find them after the war. Though I tried, I never did find them. They no longer lived at that address and in all the hustle and upheaval after the war, with so many people trying to meet up with each other, I gave up my search too easily.

I went back to my lodgings to continue planning my journey to Hungary. I knew that there was a train to the border later in the afternoon and I wanted to get going as soon as possible. I took the suitcase, some food and money and went to the railway station. The train was already at the platform; I bought a ticket and boarded the train. It was bound for Sered, quite close to the Hungarian border, from where I intended to get a taxi to take me to the closest border crossing. I was lucky, for even though it was quite late there was a taxi at the station. The driver, an old man, was very protective towards me as he drove me to the village I said was my home. By now, having already crossed the border twice, I felt quite confident that I would have no problems crossing it the third time, and my confidence was justified. After the taxi had dropped me it was but a short walk to the border. I got there around 10 o'clock in the evening so I had plenty of hours of darkness ahead of me in which to walk across comfortably. I followed all the precautions I had learned

129

before, such as watching the border guards patrolling their territory, moving immediately after they had completed their patrol, and walking silently through the villages on the other side of the border so as not to alert the dogs. I finally reached Galánta, the town from where you could get a direct train to Budapest. I thought it safer and less conspicuous to get an evening train, for most illegal travellers would take the morning train immediately after crossing the border. I couldn't spend the day at or near the station however, for railway stations were the most dangerous places. Thus I spent most of the day hiding in churches and eating in little cafés, and avoided the railway station until the last minute. Although I had had no sleep the night before, I didn't feel tired: the adrenaline was racing through my blood. I bought a ticket and surveyed the scene. I had to be careful boarding the train, for while I had Slovak papers I had no Hungarian documents. With my cheap little suitcase and shabby coat, I blended well into the crowds waiting for the train to Budapest and managed to get on the train without difficulty. I managed to get a seat and fell into a deep sleep as the exhaustion caught up with me.

9 Budapest, November– December 1944 and January 1945

It was my eighteenth birthday, 28 November 1944, when once more I returned as a refugee to Budapest. It was a cold, wet dawn, and even the mist could not obscure the shabbiness of the city. The train slowed down before reaching the capital, and I watched the grey, dirty suburbs and the pavements and roads wet from the drizzle. We were passing through a poor working class area called Köbánya, and at 6.30 in the morning it was still almost dark. The few people on the street near the railway line shuffled along resignedly, their heads bent and shoulders hunched, probably worried where food for the next day would come from. Other than that, the place seemed deserted. The train slowed down just before approaching the main railway station, and I decided that this was as good a place as any to jump off unnoticed. I knew that I had to leave the train before it reached the station because the police probably checked people's identity documents, and since I had none I would have no chance.

I opened the door of the carriage and was surprised by the height of the steps on the train. With no platform, it really was a long jump to the ground. Still, I had no option but to jump, and did so. I landed safely beside the railway line and made my way across the rails. A wire fence separated the railway line from the street, but it was quite easy to climb over it. At last I was on the street. The trams were already running as the city began to stir, and more people were in the streets. Now that I had successfully reached the outskirts of Budapest it was again time to make a decision; I had nowhere to go, and even worse, I did not know where it was safe for me to stay. I thought that I would be less conspicuous in the centre of the city, which I knew better than this part of Budapest, so I boarded a tram and with the little change I had brought with me bought a ticket to Kossúth utcza. As I watched from the tram window, I noticed how much the city had changed since I had seen it in April. The buildings were dirty, the plaster crumbling. Most shocking of all was the spectacle of a procession of Jewish people in the street.

In the grey drizzle, people wearing the yellow Star of David and pushing carts walked slowly down the middle of the road. The carts were loaded with household utensils, bedding, blankets, mattresses, etc. Some people were carrying heavy suitcases and backpacks. Many were pushing their babies in pushchairs, or carrying them in their arms. The procession consisted mainly of women, children and old people and I discovered later that they were heading towards the area designated as Budapest's ghetto. Knowing what was likely to happen to them I was moved to tears seeing them still clinging to their possessions, hoping that they would be useful to them. Clearly no news about the extermination camps had reached them, so they walked obediently to Hitler's 'final solution'. There were no young or middle-aged men in the procession; they had already been taken to so-called 'work camps', where they were supposed to help the war efforts of the retreating Hungarian army that fought alongside the German army against the Russians. These Budapest Jews were no doubt unaware that virtually all the Hungarian Jews from outside Budapest had already been deported and probably dealt with by the Germans. I did not understand at that time why the Budapest Jews had not yet been deported but were being forced to move into the ghetto. Later, it was discovered that they were pawns in a game played by Eichmann and the leaders of the Jewish community, the Jewish Council who were hoping to trade their own lives and those of some of the richest Jews for money that the Germans could use to buy weapons. The others were herded into the ghetto where they would be exterminated before the Germans retreated from Budapest. I was painfully aware that these Jews who were walking towards the ghetto were unaware of the contents of Walter's report, which he had so painstakingly put together and smuggled in to Hungary to warn about the liquidation of Jews in Auschwitz and other camps. This information had been kept secret by the treacherous leaders of the Jewish community, and had procured the complacency and peaceful obedience of these people.

I had to abandon my concern and thoughts about the round-up of Jews on the streets because I had my own pressing problems to solve. Although I hadn't yet reached my destination, I couldn't sit any longer in the tram; I wanted to get out. I stepped out at the next stop and enjoyed walking in the cold fresh air. To get a proper feel of the city I needed to walk the streets, to feel the hard surface of the pavement, sniff the air and mingle with the people. The pathetic procession of the unsuspecting Jews had filled me with anger and strengthened my determination to live and to try to do as much as possible to save some of these people. But to be able to do anything I needed help myself.

How could I live, when there was nowhere for me to go and stay, and what could I do with no identity papers and little money? I had to find some place where I could spend at least the first day and night. I crossed the Margaret Bridge and walked towards my cousin's house in Buda, where I had stayed for a while before leaving for Slovakia in April earlier in the year. It seemed strange, almost impossible, that only six months before I had walked these same streets almost without fear, in total ignorance of what was happening in the concentration camps. Now I was cautious as I surveyed the surroundings. There was a surprising number of official-looking cars, and on closer inspection I saw that several German officers were coming and going from my cousin's house. There was no sign of my cousin, or any members of the family. The Germans must have confiscated the house, to provide lodgings, or maybe offices for their officers. What had happened to my cousin Baby? I couldn't expect an answer to that question here and it was dangerous to hang about outside the house.

Although it was only the middle of the afternoon, it got dark early at this time of year. I guessed there was a curfew, so it was dangerous to be out in the dark. Moreover, there would be no lights anywhere in the city after dusk, because Budapest was a target for bombing and there would be a complete blackout. So, not only would it be dangerous, but it would also be difficult to wander about in the dark. Suddenly I had an idea about where I might spend the night. During previous summers I had often gone canoeing with my aunt and I remembered that on the embankment of the Danube there were several huts where the canoes were kept. One of these huts, no doubt abandoned at this time of year, might be a good hiding place for a night or two. So I walked along the embankment for about 3 km, past Margaret Island to the place on the outskirts of Budapest where I remembered these huts were. I found the place, and tried to open the door of a few of them. They were all locked up for the winter. I had nearly given up when I discovered that the door of one of the huts was unlocked. I went into the hut, leaving the door ajar to get some light, and had a look inside. I could see canoes and life jackets. It was freezing cold and I had no blanket, no spare warm clothes and the thin navy coat that I wore would not be enough to protect me from the cold. Maybe a life jacket could help. I found one that fitted me and put it on to keep me warm. Thus dressed, I settled under a canoe, which too provided some protection from the cold.

Before I fell asleep, I tried to make a list of my options and errands that I had to do the next day. I desperately wanted news of my father, who I thought was still somewhere in Hungary in a work camp. As I was trying to get to sleep I felt ravenous and realized that I hadn't eaten all day, but it was too late to do anything about it. Finally I curled up, fell asleep and slept until dawn.

I got up early in the morning and felt quite refreshed. There was a water tap outside the hut; fortunately there was no one around and I quickly splashed some cold water over my face. I was starving, and badly needed to get some money to buy food. I set out to find my relatives' flat, for even more important than money and food was information about my father and what was going on with the Jews in Budapest, so that I could plan my next move. Thus, in spite of some hesitation and worry about jeopardizing my Aunt Manci's safety by visiting her, I set out to find her.

Manci lived in a large apartment in a street close to the Margaret Bridge. I walked back along the shores of the Danube, crossed the Margaret Bridge from Buda to Pest and found the apartment block. On the gate there was a big notice: 'Protected by the Swedish Government.' I didn't know what it meant, but thought that it couldn't be a bad thing. So I went up to the second floor to my aunt's apartment. I rang her doorbell and to my great joy she came to the door and let me in. She was surprised to see me, but then in those times nothing was that extraordinary. It was wonderful to find her, though she looked pale and very tired. Her face lit up with pleasure, and she pulled me into the hall. It was a very emotional moment; we embraced and kissed. Manci's happiness was contagious and her radiant smile made me feel that this was the turning point and that my troubles would soon be over. She led me into the sitting room, and just being back there, seated on the green sofa below the large painting of a nude lady, where I had spent so many happy hours with Manci discussing all sorts of problems, made me feel full of hope. Manci realized that I was hungry, and produced a cup of some warm liquid and something to eat. Then she looked at me questioningly and asked: 'Where is your mother? Why did you come back here from Slovakia? As you can see, things are very bad here.' Before telling her what had happened to us, I asked: 'Manci, where is my father?' Manci smiled, because at least she could give me some good news: 'He was here yesterday, but had to go back to his unit. He is fine, he works in the kitchen so he's not starving. Also he is pleased that you and your mother are safe. But now tell me what happened?' She went to the kitchen to get some more food for me and I followed her. It was good to see that little had changed in the flat. The chequered tiles in the kitchen were spotlessly clean and only the white kitchen cabinets were shabbier than when I had last seen them a few months ago. She found some more bread and cheese and put it on a plate for me. While I was watching her I started to tell her what happened to my mother, Martin and Grandma at the Gestapo. I was ashamed to tell her about my escape, but she was very controlled as she listened. We returned to the sitting room and sat down on the comfortable sofa. Manci told me some more good news. Most of our family in Budapest were in hiding, and safe. 'Andor [Manci's husband],' she said, 'is in a work camp like your father, but he too is fine and alive.'

I was devastated that had I missed my father by one day, for although it was good to hear that he was alive and reasonably well, I did have a premonition that I would never see him again. Manci was optimistic about her own situation, though as it turned out later, this optimism was not quite justified. Apparently the Jewish families living in this house had somehow managed to obtain some protection from the Swedish Embassy, and as a result of this protection they were to be left in their apartments and not taken away. There were two other families living in Manci's flat so it was quite crowded, but she nevertheless asked me to stay with her. I would have loved to stay but I couldn't accept her invitation. I had no documents and without documents I might endanger her and the others in the apartment; the Hungarian police carried out frequent unexpected checks on the documents of people living in the 'protected houses'. But I also wanted to be free to find some groups of young people who were involved in clandestine activities. However, Manci's warm welcome and initial help of food and some money allowed me to start organizing my life.

First I had to find someone to help me arrange my new

identity, but that would take time. In the meantime, I needed a safe place to stay for a few days. I tried to remember all the people I had met and known during my previous stay in Budapest, when I lived there with my parents. I recalled that during that time I had taken some French lessons. My teacher, Kismartony Anker Mária, was a delightful young Hungarian woman with liberal views. Her family was an old Hungarian family with close links to the Horthy government. I decided to go and visit her and ask her for help and advice.

To reach Mária I had to get across the Elisabeth Bridge to get to Buda. Her apartment was in a shabby block under the Gellért Hill, close to the elegant Gellért Hotel. I walked through the centre of the town, crossed the Elisabeth Bridge and found the address without difficulty. Now I had to be careful not to be seen by the concierge, who was likely to be an informer, and I didn't want to cause Mária any trouble. I managed to sneak into the building unobserved, climbed the stairs to the second floor and found the door to Mária's apartment.

Mária was a rare breed of Hungarian woman. Though she came from a semi-aristocratic background and was attractive, she was unmarried, and earned her living by giving French lessons to students. As I rang the bell, I wasn't sure how she would react to me. Mária opened the door. When she saw me she gave me a broad smile, as though she was expecting me. 'What brings you here?' she asked, as she let me in. I briefly told her what had happened to me and my parents. She listened attentively and was sympathetic. 'It is quite embarrassing but true that the Hungarians, by being Germany's allies also have responsibility for the Nazis' inhuman behaviour,' she said. Then she asked: 'What can I do to help?'

I explained that I had nowhere to stay and needed accommodation and time to find my friends who might help me. 'Could I stay with you for a few days?' I finally managed to ask. She looked at me in a way that made me feel I had embarrassed her. After a brief pause she said: 'Look, Gerti, I would love to help you, but you can't stay here, because I am already hiding three French refugees who've escaped from a prisoner of war camp. I think it would be too difficult for me to have another person.' I felt very dejected, and it must have shown, because Mária suddenly said: 'I have an idea. My brother has a big villa in Rózsadomb and he lives alone with a house-keeper. Maybe he would agree to have you. How about that?' I was a bit worried because I didn't know Mária's brother and was not sure how safe I would be there. But I had no option, so I accepted her proposal. Mária phoned her brother and he agreed to give me shelter for a few days. Then she gave me instructions about how to get to his villa and told me that the housekeeper would be told that I was a visiting relative from the country. She told me what name I should use, and gave me the name of the town I was supposed to come from. Finally she asked: 'Do you have any suitcase, or clothes, because you'd expect a visitor should have them.' I had only a small bag that contained soap, a toothbrush and a small towel, and nothing to wear apart from the things I had on. Mária, who was about the same size as me said: 'I will put something together for you – a nightdress, a blouse and a skirt and a few other bits and pieces.' She then produced a small suitcase and filled it with some of her clothes and underwear. I was deeply moved by her kindness and generosity, which I accepted gladly.

Equipped with the suitcase and yet another temporary fictional identity, I set off towards my new destination. Following Mária's instructions, I took the tram and bus close to the address she gave me. Mária's brother's villa was in one of the most prestigious parts of the city and I felt completely out of place there. It was a most luxurious villa, surrounded by trees and gardens. I knew that Mária's brother was an important civil servant at the ministry of defence, but I hadn't expected that he would live in such luxury. I rang the bell and the housekeeper, a pleasant-looking woman in her forties, opened the door. She greeted me with a friendly smile: 'I was expecting you. Sir Anker phoned and asked me to prepare the guest room for you and take care of you because he will be back late tonight. You must be tired after the journey – I hear the trains are slow and transport disrupted, because the Russian troops are getting nearer and all the transport is used for the army. How was the journey?' I was a little embarrassed, for according to my new identity I was supposed to have come from the eastern part of Hungary close to where the fighting was taking place. 'It was slow, as you said, but I got here in the end, and I am glad to be with my relatives.' The housekeeper said: 'My name is Szylvia, and I come from a village outside Szeged. I worry about my family there – it's near the front. What is your name?' 'Éva Takács.'

She took my suitcase and we went up to the first floor. There she opened one of the doors and showed me into a wonderfully cosy little room. 'This is the guest room. You can make yourself comfortable here. The bathroom is just across the corridor and the water is hot, ready for a bath.' The thought of a hot bath overshadowed all the other surprises and impressions of the luxury that surrounded me. Szylvia brought me a glass of espresso coffee and a slice of apple strudel on a tray. She put it on my bedside table and left. I sat down on the bed, which had cool, clean sheets, and wasn't quite sure whether or not I was dreaming all this. The prospect of the bath was still the greatest attraction of all, so I went into the bathroom. There was indeed plenty of hot water, also wonderfully scented soap and soft towels, kept warm by the radiators. In fact the whole house was comfortably warm. When I had finished my bath I went straight to bed and fell asleep.

It was late evening when Szylvia knocked at my door and woke me to tell me that dinner was ready and that Sir Anker (my fictional uncle) was expecting me. So I got ready and went to the dining room anxious to make a favourable impression on my host. The dining room, like the rest of the house, was tastefully furnished, and an exquisite chandelier made of bohemian crystal was hanging above the large dining table. My host was a tall, slim man, with thick brown hair and a moustache. There was some physical resemblance between him and his sister, but he seemed much more serious. When we were alone he introduced himself: 'I am Aristid and I understand that you are Éva'. He had a pleasant manner and very warm smile. 'I hope that Szylvia looked after you properly,' he added. I felt very embarrassed and didn't know what to say. Finally I stammered: 'I hope that I will not inconvenience you for long, I will try to sort something out soon.' He smiled back at me, and said: 'Maybe I can help you to sort something out, I have access to information about those parts of Hungary that are now occupied by the Russians. There are many refugees from that part of the country, particularly right-wing members of the Szálasy (Arrow Cross) party and those involved in helping the Germans to deport the Jews and fight the Russians. There is a special committee set up here in Budapest that looks after these refugees and gives them support, accommodation and all they need. I could get you enough information for you to pose as one of those. You do not look Jewish, or like a gypsy – you're good-looking and very young. That will appeal to the officials who decide whom to help. You also look quite innocent, but perhaps you could just make yourself look a bit more helpless. Do you want me to find out more about it for you?'

To me this seemed a brilliant idea. To be looked after by the Hungarian fascists and supported by them was bizarre and, at the same time, truly wonderful. Perhaps others could benefit from all this, too. 'I'd be very grateful if you could find out for me how to get such support,' I replied to my host. 'Agreed,' he said. 'There is nothing else we can do tonight, so let's tell Szylvia to serve us dinner, then we can have a chat and get to know each other a little.' The dinner was not only excellent but served on beautiful Herendi porcelain dishes. We ate with silver cutlery. It reminded me of my aunt's house as a child, yet for me now this setting seemed quite unreal. To be here, surrounded by this luxury after all the nights and days that I had spent roughing it outdoors and in most unpleasant places, seemed like a dream.

When we had finished our dinner I asked my host whether

I could borrow a book to read, the ultimate luxury. He took me to his study and showed me his books. I chose a book by a Hungarian writer I was particularly fond of called Karinthy Frigyes. His style was rather amusing, and I felt that it would be a pleasant distraction. I borrowed the book and bid my host goodnight.

In 'my' room I went to bed, switched on my bedside light and read my book until I was ready to sleep. Next morning I woke to the sound of someone knocking on my door. It was Szylvia who asked what I wanted for breakfast. Tea, coffee, poached eggs or just toast and butter with jam? I said I wanted coffee and everything else. She gave me a slightly surprised look, but didn't make any further comments. A little later, my breakfast arrived on a trolley, beautifully served. It tasted absolutely delicious. I had forgotten that food could taste as good as the dinner I'd had the night before, and this breakfast; and the luxury of having breakfast served in bed! If I die now, at least I had one day of good living, I thought. Yet I couldn't entirely submerge myself in these pleasures. The images of my parents, and the nagging feeling of uncertainty about them never left me. I also felt very guilty for not having saved them and taken care of them. But there was nothing I could do about that part of my situation, so I decided to enjoy myself as much as I could.

Szylvia told me that Sir Anker would return from work early that afternoon and would like to talk to me and then take me out in the evening. It seemed natural to Szylvia that he was keen to spend some time with his niece.

I put on a dress that Mária had packed in my little suitcase and looked quite respectable. When my host arrived he said: 'We'd better have a talk now.' He took some papers out of his briefcase and showed me a map of Eastern Hungary. He pointed to a spot near Nyiregyháza and said: 'There is a tiny village here called Ludas. It has only about 100 inhabitants, so the chances that you might run into another refugee from there are small. Still, I have to brief you about the village, because the committee that gives help to refugees will want quite a lot of detail from you to make sure that you truly are a refugee. Since you have no papers you have to be extremely well briefed.' He pulled out another map, this time of the village. On the map he showed me the main street, the church and the shops, then he wrote down the names of various people who lived in the village – the priest, the butcher, shopkeeper – and other details about the place. He said: 'You could call yourself Éva Jurkovics. A family of that name with a daughter your age lived just behind the church. The family also had a son and a father in the army so they're unlikely to turn up. The father was a staunch supporter of Szálasy. You also have a younger, 10-year-old sister, and you should claim that your mother didn't want to leave the village on her account, but encouraged you to leave and flee the Russian army, which has already occupied the village, and many Russian soldiers raped young girls and women.' When he had finished giving me all this information and advice, we went out to dinner to a small *csárda* (inn) in Buda. Had I not experienced it, I would not have believed it possible that there were still places in Budapest where good food was available in such a luxurious atmosphere. 'Well I guess tomorrow you will depart and try your luck with the refugee office. Learn your story well, and I will test you in the morning,' said Mr Anker.

After dinner we returned to the villa and I settled down to learn the details of my new identity, past and family. I slept fitfully and kept waking up and repeating my new name to myself. In the morning after breakfast, my host came into my room and tested me thoroughly. He was reasonably well pleased with my performance, and we said goodbye to each other. He went to work and I went to the refugee office with my little suitcase.

There was a long queue, and I had to wait for a long time until finally my turn came. I was asked all the questions about myself that I had rehearsed with Mr Anker the night before. They asked me why I had fled, where I lived, the names of the people I knew in the village. Apparently my performance was quite satisfactory, because I was given refugee status, documents, an apartment in Buda and a weekly allowance that was quite generous. I was beside myself with delight. I was taken by one of the employees of this organization, which looked after fascist refugees, to my new apartmentt. It was in Buda, close to the river. It was on the fourth floor, and the lift was working. I reached my new front door and opened it using the key I had been given. I entered a spacious hall. There were four rooms, a well-equipped kitchen and a clean bathroom. It was evidently a luxury apartment that had belonged to someone who had fled from Budapest to Vienna, in fear of the Russian army. The furniture was nearly new, and functional. I couldn't believe my luck and was much amused by the irony of it. After all, the fascists had supported me and unwittingly given me a chance. I promised myself that I would use it. Since I had hardly any possessions there was no need to move anything. All I had to do was become acquainted with the contents of the apartment, which were now mine to use. But I felt lonely and forlorn and very, very tired.

MY NEW LIFE ALONE

Next day I started my new life. I had remembered the phone number of a Jewish boy who worked for the Zionists, which had been given to me by Dov in Bratislava before I left for Hungary. Now that I was safely installed I set out to contact him. I called the number and after a lot of cross-examination to make sure that it was safe to meet, we agreed to meet on the corner of Kossúth utcza and Váczi utcza in the inner city.

My new contact was very secretive when we met on the street, and would not disclose his address. He told me that he was involved in forging documents and then giving them to someone who took them into the Ghetto to get people out of there. I explained to him who I was and that I had managed to get a large apartment and a safe identity, and that I would like to help the Jewish people in Budapest. 'To start with, I can

143

at least offer accommodation to some of the fugitives and members of the group that need somewhere to stay,' I said to him. 'Would you be prepared to carry forged documents to the ghetto so that those of our friends who got taken there can get out?' he asked. 'Then perhaps they could stay in your flat for a few days until we find something for them.'

I agreed, and this is how my career as a courier started. I became very involved, and quite skilled at carrying suitcases filled with forged papers into the Ghetto. I was a suitable person for this task, being blonde and plump. With a blue ribbon in my hair, I looked like a typical Aryan teenager, whose father might indeed have been a concierge in one of the apartment blocks, who had had to move out of the Ghetto and vacate the apartment to make way for the Jews. My excuse for entering the Ghetto was that I had to pick up some of our possessions, which we had not yet moved.

The Ghetto was terribly overcrowded. Several families shared a single room and facilities such as bathrooms, kitchens, etc., were completely inadequate. It was of course infested with lice, fleas and bedbugs. There was a shortage of food, but at least there was still a good supply of water.

Before I went to the Ghetto with my suitcase full of forged papers, I always had to memorize the names and addresses of the people to whom the papers had to be handed over. My contacts were usually young Zionists who had been taken to the Ghetto and organized the distribution of the papers there. On my way out I filled up my suitcase with junk, kitchen utensils, etc., so that I could pass through the sentry and show the things I had picked up. At each visit I had to be careful not to bump into the same person who had manned a sentry during an earlier visit. Thus I would stand for a long while at the entrance to the Ghetto and watch the guards. I was extremely lucky that I was never caught, or even suspected. Instead, I was often asked out by the guards, and had to tell them stories of my strict parents who would not allow me to go out with a man. I think that, too, impressed them.

MANCI'S STORY

During this period, in early December 1944, many Jews were marched on foot across Hungary to the Austrian border and then taken over by the Gestapo to end up in some of the concentration camps that were still functioning. It was a bitterly cold winter, and the 60 km march took at least three days and nights, without any shelter day or night. The ordeal was too much for many of the people, particularly the children. Being taken on such a march was therefore bad news, and the chances that anyone who was not young and fit would return were slim. Not for nothing were the marches called 'death marches'.

One day I went to visit my Aunt Manci in the block of apartments that was supposedly protected by the Swedish consulate in Budapest. When I approached the building, however, I noticed that the notice board proclaiming that the Jews who lived there were under Swedish protection had been removed. I subsequently discovered that my aunt's flat was empty. I knew this meant that she had been taken either into the Ghetto or on one of the death marches. From then on, I kept searching the Ghetto for my aunt or anyone who would be able to give me some information about her. Finally I struck lucky, for there she was in one of the overcrowded flats, looking terribly thin and distraught and apathetic. When she saw me, I had to explain to her who I was, for she didn't recognize me in my smart coat, all made up to look pretty. She took a while to believe me, but in the end she was glad to see me alive and well. However, she would not cooperate with me when I suggested that I could take her out of the Ghetto. She was too apathetic to try.

She described her ordeal to me. One day a group of Hungarian militia men came to her apartment block and claimed that everyone had to get ready for a long march to the Austrian border, because the Swedish protection was no longer valid. Luckily, she thought to put on her warmest clothing, and good walking boots, which probably saved her life. Then like many others from similar blocks, including children and old people, she was marched to the Austrian border, and it was hell. They walked during the day, and slept in the open during the night. It took three days and two nights to reach the border. All they received by way of food was some hot thin soup and a piece of bread. Those who couldn't walk were shot by the roadside. Manci survived the march because she was quite fit, had good warm clothing and good boots. At the border they began to prepare the handover of the surviving Jews to the Gestapo, but a Swedish official who was standing on a stool shouted through the loudspeaker that those Jews who had Swedish protection and evidence of it should be returned to Budapest. The Swede, as it turned out, was Raoul Wallenberg, who saved many Hungarian Jews. Tragically, when Hungary was liberated by the Russians Wallenberg was arrested; he died in a Stalinist gulag. But for many Hungarian Jews whose lives he saved through his great personal courage he will always remain a legend. My aunt had her Swedish document in her pocket and duly produced it. She was then directed to a different queue, given food and drink and marched back to Budapest, but this time at a gentler pace with stops to eat and drink. However, on her arrival in Budapest, she was not sent back to her apartment but put into the Ghetto. She showed me how dirty she was, and told me she had got lice. The Ghetto was also riddled with fleas and bedbugs. Manci was a very fastidious lady, and this indignity of dirt, lice, fleas and bedbugs completely demoralized her.

In the end, I persuaded her to allow me to take her out of the Ghetto and said that she could then either stay with me, or if it was safe, return to her apartment block. I filled in a forged birth certificate making out she was my mother, then saw to her appearance. She had a smart coat, but her trouser legs, which showed beneath the knees, were in tatters. I managed to get her to hitch up her trouser legs so that they didn't show, since she didn't want to take them off. I then put some make-up on her face to make her look less worn out and despondent and took my suitcase with the few of her possessions that were in a reasonable state. Then I took her arm and pretended to be cheerful as I chatted to her and walked out past the guards. No one stopped us, and my aunt thought this was incredible. But I knew that if you pretended to be happy and carefree, and joked with the guards, you stood a good chance of not being taken for a Ghetto Jew. We went to Manci's apartment. The notice saying that the inhabitants were under Swedish protection had reappeared, but hardly any of the old tenants were there. To our surprise, however, her husband was there, released from his work camp. He told us that it was perfectly safe for my aunt to stay there.

BACK IN MY FLAT

I returned to my apartment in Buda. By then, there were several young people staying with me there. Most of them stayed only for a night or two, but three of them were there almost permanently: two boys, Józska and Mishka, and a girl, Lea. We all worked together, trying to rescue as many people from being deported as possible, and a deep friendship developed between the four of us. I looked forward to seeing them in the evening after a tiring day. Time had passed quickly and it was now the middle of December.

One evening, as I was approaching the apartment, I could hear gun fire quite close. To me it was the most delightful music, for it showed that the Russians had started their offensive in Buda, and meant that we might soon be free of the Germans. On the streets there were abandoned army trucks and this evening, just outside the building where our apartment was, there was a crowd of people trying to carve up a dead horse. I tried not to look and went inside quickly. I, too, was very hungry; we hadn't seen meat for weeks, but we were not too keen to take part in the dissection of the horse. I entered the apartment and only Lea was home. She offered me some very welcome warm soup – we had no heating in the flat, unless we had managed to find some wood on the street or on the river bank. However, we hadn't yet got to the stage where we burned furniture, doors, etc. After supper I wrapped myself up and went to bed putting on all the warm clothes I could find, too cold to undress.

I must have slept very soundly, for when I woke up next morning I was covered in soot, broken plaster and bricks and a lot of dust. At first I didn't quite realize what had happened, but then I saw that the wall of my room that faced the street had a great hole in it. Fortunately, my bed was on the other side of the room, otherwise I would have been dead. The house must have been hit by a bullet or shell from a Russian gun. I crept out of bed, shook off some of the dust and looked for my flatmates. Everyone else seemed to have survived the shelling and only my room had been hit. But it was a lucky hit, for all the doors to those rooms that the previous owners had locked were blown ajar by the pressure of the blast. One room was a large storage room which contained enormous supplies of food: various tins with meat, rice and flour. This was a wonderful surprise and we decided to have a celebratory feast. The only problem was water. We had to go to a tap on the street some distance away to fetch it, and that meant risking our lives, because the shelling had by now resumed and intensified. Still, we were so delighted that Buda at last was under siege and that the Germans would soon have to leave the city that we didn't really care. So we went out, got some water and prepared our feast. We had a really great evening, with tinned Hungarian goulash, big plates of rice and wine, all from the open store room of our fascist landlords.

Now that we had enough food, life in our apartment seemed quite luxurious and all of us looked forward to returning to it from our various quite dangerous assignments during the next few weeks. Józska was always remote, and kept very much to himself. Mishka on the other hand was a cheerful boy with a great sense of humour, very good at telling stories and jokes. We liked each other very much. One evening,

Mishka and I were alone in the apartment. We were sitting next to each other on a sofa and discussing the day's events. Unexpectedly, Mishka put his arm around my shoulders and drew me close. As I looked into his face, he put his lips to mine and tried to kiss me. I was confused, for I had never thought of him as a potential lover, or boyfriend. I felt no desire to have a physical relationship with him. But he said that he loved me very much, and argued that for both of us this might be the only chance we had to experience what love-making was all about. 'We may be dead tomorrow, and if we don't try now we may never know what it is like to make love to a person you desire.' He said many other things, but somehow nothing seemed to me to be a good enough reason to force myself into an action I did not particularly want, for I did not feel any compulsion to make love to him, or for that matter to anyone else at that particularly harrowing time. So I quite firmly rejected him, something I was to regret for the rest of my life.

When Christmas came, the four of us 'celebrated' Christmas together. It was around Christmas however that we noticed with dismay that the Russians had stopped their shelling and their offensive on Buda. Thus the war for us was not yet over and survival was still uncertain. The year 1944 departed but the end of our fight had not arrived.

LEA'S STORY

One cold evening at the beginning of January 1945, when I was alone in our apartment, I heard a knock at the door. I was worried that some unexpected visitors might have found me, since my flatmates all had a key. Also it was past curfew, and my friends were not yet at home. So with great trepidation I went to the door and looked through the peephole. And there was Lea, naked, disshevelled and with her hands tied behind her back. I was scared that she might have been followed by the police but my response was nevertheless swift – I opened the door and dragged her in. She was half-unconscious from

149

cold and exposure, but after a few hot drinks and sitting wrapped up in a warm blanket she gradually recovered and was able to tell her story.

'Just before curfew the three of us Mishka, Józska and I were returning home to our apartment, from a meeting with our friends in Pest, where we discussed possible strategies for helping Jews out of the Ghetto and hiding them. We had just crossed the *Lánc hid* [chain bridge], when a group of about ten Hungarian militiamen asked for our identity papers. As you know, we had quite good forged papers, identifying all of us as Hungarians who had fled the advancing Russian army. The Hungarian militiamen were drunk, didn't really examine the papers and tried to separate me from the boys. Mishka and Józska were worried about me and tried to stop the soldiers from dragging me away. This annoyed the Hungarians. They turned on the two young boys, surrounded them and shouted abuse at them. One of the Hungarians, no older than 18 and very aggressive, screamed: "You better show us your pricks, I bet you are Jewish pigs, or you wouldn't mind a girl to be of service to the Hungarian patriotic front." Then they forced the two boys to take down their pants, and of course discovered that they were circumcised. Delighted at having captured three victims, they started beating and mocking us. They tied our hands with a rope behind our backs and we were forced to walk along the river bank. The militiamen were exhilarated with their "success", they sung, shouted and made obscene proposals to me. Finally we reached a spot on the river bank where other Jews were already lined up, presumably ready to be shot. We were the last ones to arrive. Then everything happened very fast. A gun was pointed at us, the militiamen untied our hands and ordered us to strip naked. When we stood there stripped naked in the freezing cold our hands were tied again. The Hungarians enjoyed watching us shivering in the cold and they took their time organizing the next step, shooting us into the cold river. We were ordered to line up at the river bank, facing the river. Then two of the militiamen started to shoot their victims. The bodies fell and sank under the thin ice. Those that didn't quite fall into the river were pushed in. By this time it was getting dark and the total black-out in Budapest meant you couldn't see much. I was the last in the row and by the time my turn came it was completely dark. I had had some time to prepare myself and the darkness helped. When my turn came I pretended to be shot and hurled myself in the freezing Danube just before the bullet that was meant to kill me hit me. I stayed in the icy water for a while, then swam a short distance to the river bank. No one seemed to have seen me as I climbed out on the river bank – I was hidden by the darkness. I was near to losing consciousness from the cold, but I forced myself to stay hidden under a bush until the militiamen went away. I don't know how I managed to stay still feeling so desperately cold, but I was so frightened that I waited as long as I could. When I could no longer stand the cold I started to walk very fast through the dark deserted streets of Budapest, naked with my hands tied behind my back. It really is a miracle that I got here, and now I don't know how I will survive the pain.'

I wondered whether Lea would ever manage to recover from her ordeal. She was just 17 years old, and she too came from Slovakia. Both her parents had been taken to a concentration camp and she had had no news of them. Mishka, Józska and I were her family and now two of us were dead and she had witnessed their murder.

Although we knew that many Jews had lost their lives in this way, and we were aware of the risks we were taking by doing our job, it was nevertheless extremely difficult to come to terms with the fact that we had lost two of our best friends.

In addition to the grief at our loss, I felt guilty. I couldn't stop thinking about Mishka and the last few days of his life. I remembered with remorse that evening when we had been alone in our apartment, and he had sat next to me, drawn me towards him and tried to kiss me. I hadn't desired him and had rejected him without giving any thought to how much it would have meant to him. Now that he was dead it seemed a terrible thing to have done. It would have done me no harm to make love to him and he would have had at least something he badly wanted in his short life.

Lea and I talked all night about what to do next. The searches for Jews with forged papers were getting more and more thorough and the Russians were not advancing rapidly enough on to Buda, where we lived. Maybe it was time to move on to the other side of the river to Pest, where the Russian Army was making more progress. The bridges connecting the two parts of the town were to be destroyed and if we wanted to move to Pest we had to do it fast. We collected some warm clothing, put it into a backpack and started our walk through the deserted, wounded city. Every house was pockmarked with bullet holes, the streets were deserted, and there were signs of death everywhere. Remnants of carcasses of dead animals stripped bare by hungry people littered the streets. It was a devastating sight. We chose to walk across Elisabeth (Erzsébet) Bridge, since it was the most beautiful and led straight to the heart of Pest. Naively we thought that this might make the bridge less likely to be destroyed. At the same time, we were afraid that the bridge was already mined and might explode at any time. We reached the other side safely, but the bridge was destroyed about two hours after we had crossed it.

LIBERATION BY THE RUSSIANS

We had an address to go to in case we needed help. It was the headquarters of the Zionist group of Jewish boys and girls who had produced the forged papers that I had carried to the Ghetto. It was in Benczúr street, just off the main boulevard in Pest, the famous Andrássy út with its many exquisite houses, which included the Opera House.

When we arrived at our destination there were only a few young people there. Most of them had gone out to watch the street fighting. We had a little rest, a hot drink of some sort, and after a while Lea and I decided that we, too, would watch the fighting. We went towards the city park (Városliget), from where we could hear a lot of noise and shooting. The park was quite near the place where we were now staying. On the way, the streets were full of tanks containing weary German soldiers. We reached the park, where a lot of fighting was going on. We didn't know anything about the Russians, except that we hoped that they would not be as dangerous to us as the Germans, and that was enough for us to give them all our sympathy. This, then, was our first encounter with the mighty Russian army that was chasing the Germans out of their own and other occupied countries. We hid behind a big tree and watched. The Russian soldiers were standing completely unprotected and exposed, occasionally firing their machine guns, but their targets were concealed. The German soldiers, camouflaged and protected by trees and bushes, were shooting with deadly accuracy at the exposed Russian soldiers, who were toppling over like marionettes. As they did so, others took their place with a seeming equal lack of concern and a carelessness, as though life was not of great value to them. Lea and I watched the spectacle with fascination. The scene seemed quite unreal and yet was very disturbing. We felt like crying out and warning the Russians, 'Please take cover, the war is nearly over, don't die now,' but there was nothing we could do. I decided that I couldn't watch this any longer and went back alone, since Lea wanted to see what happened and who was going to take over the park.

I walked to our new lodgings and noticed a damaged, abandoned German tank at the entry to our street. This was nothing new, so I continued on my way. Our room was on the first floor, so I climbed up the stairs and it was then to my amazement that I saw a young German soldier huddled outside the door. I should have been frightened, but he looked so dejected: when he saw me he turned his childish blue eyes towards me and asked in German whether he could get a glass of water. I let him into our room and into the kitchen, which was quite comfortable and warm. He took off his belt and the holster with his pistol. He then told me that he was the only remaining person from the crew that manned the tank at the entrance of the street. His other comrades had been killed and he was completely exhausted. When he told me that he was just 18, the same age as me, I believed him. I was not sure what to do. Here I was, alone, facing an enemy whom I could easily kill with his pistol, so carelessly left on the table, which would have meant that the tank would no longer be a threat to the fighting Russians who had to sacrifice their lives as they entered every street defended by the Germans. When I looked at the soldier sitting there, unsuspecting, sipping from the glass I had handed him, I knew that the right thing to do was to take the pistol and kill him, but I couldn't make myself do it. I had never killed anyone, and all the violence and killing I had had to witness made such an act even more repulsive than it would otherwise have been. So I let him finish his drink, retrieve his pistol and walk out towards the tank. When he left I followed to see what happened. He reached the tank and a group of Russian soldiers tried to ambush it. Several shots were fired, and three Russian soldiers were left either wounded or dead. Then the Russians threw a grenade at the tank and it exploded, killing the young German soldier. So by my squeamishness, I sacrificed three lives unnecessarily. I felt nauseated and ashamed for my lack of resolve to use the pistol, or at least to disarm the German and keep him harmless in our flat, though I knew that was impossible, for when the rest of our group returned they would not have hesitated to kill him.

Finally, when night came, Lea and the three boys who had been in the apartment when we arrived and had allowed us to stay there returned from the street with rumours that probably by morning Pest would be liberated by the Russians and that all the bridges had already been blown up by the Germans. Apparently agreement had been reached that the Jewish Ghetto, which the Germans had planned to destroy, would not be blown up and the people in the Ghetto would be liberated tomorrow.

We talked a little more with these boys, who we didn't know well. The oldest, József, was about 22 years old, had blond hair, blue eyes and was very German looking. He told us that he sometimes impersonated German Gestapo officers and often helped to free Jews who had been captured by the Gestapo. I admired him and thought that he was very clever and brave. The other boy was called András and was a little younger. He helped to find food and water for members of the group and also helped with forging various documents. The third boy, Sándor, was about 17 years old and very shy. He was of small build and rather delicate. I don't know exactly what he was doing in the group, but I think he was a sort of scout who could watch unobserved and keep the group informed as to who was approaching the house. That night we were very excited as we went to sleep, hoping that this would be our last night in German occupied Europe.

Throughout the night the noise of the gunfire didn't stop, but it didn't keep us awake. We were so used to it that it had become part of the environment in which we lived. Next morning, the street was occupied by Russian soldiers and we were at last free.

10 January–May 1945

On 15 January the fighting in our street had stopped. The apartment in Benczúr utcza looked abandoned. It was littered with papers, dirty cups and plates. Most of the people who had stayed or worked there had left and only five people remained: József, András, Sándor, Lea and I. We discussed what to do next. József, the oldest of us, proposed that we should leave Budapest and move further away from the fighting, because the Germans might return to Pest and the fighting could start again. We agreed that it would be safer to move away to a place where the Russian army had been for longer and where life might be more settled. András, Sándor and Lea thought we should move immediately, and pointed out that it will be difficult to obtain food, coal or any other essential supplies in Budapest. Also the state of the apartment was depressing, and we had no inclination to stay and make it habitable. The clandestine activities we had had to carry out in order to survive were closely linked to the apartment and we longed to put this experience behind us. Leaving Budapest might help our recovery, and we wanted to do so immediately. József was worried about coming with us. He thought that he might put us in danger because he was still wearing the German army greatcoat he used when he pretended to be a German officer to pull our friends out of the work camp. In his coat and together with his blond hair and Germanic looks, the Russians would surely take him for a German, capture

him, and perhaps us as well. 'You go without me and I will go
by myself and meet you later,' he said. But we didn't want to
split up, and argued that we needed his advice and help.
Finally we searched the apartment, found some less conspicuous clothes for him to wear, and with a cap to hide his blond
hair we made him look more like a Jewish boy returning from
work camp, rather than a German.

The next problem was deciding where to go. We had a map
of Hungary and we studied it carefully. We wanted to choose
a place big enough to find work, shelter, relative peace and
enough food. Finally, after much deliberation, we decided to
go to a town by the Tisza River south of Budapest called
Szeged. Szeged had a good university, so we expected to find
many young people living there. It was also in the middle of
fertile land, which promised a good food supply. None of us
had many belongings, so it didn't take us long to pack and get
ready.

There was no question as to the means of transport: there
were no trains running and no buses either. We would have to
walk and, if possible, hitch a ride from the Russian soldiers.
We knew nothing about our Russian liberators but had
complete confidence that they would be helpful.

It was a bitterly cold day. There was fresh snow on the
roads, which of course had not been cleared away, so we
waded knee deep in it. It was difficult to see the road, but
fortunately, in built up areas it was not too hard to find our
way. To our surprise, the streets were completely empty, with
not a living soul to be seen, and the houses we passed seemed
abandoned. Only very seldom did we see some Russian
soldiers strolling among the houses, carrying bags or parcels.
Nobody stopped us or talked to us, and the silence was eerie.
We followed the road signs towards a town called Szolnok,
which was on the way to Szeged and was connected to
Budapest by a major road. By the time we reached the
outskirts of Budapest we were cold and hungry. 'Shall we find
out what is happening and why there are no people on the
street?' Lea suggested, and we agreed to knock on some

doors. However, the snow had not been cleared in any of the driveways, and there were no footprints leading to the entrance of the houses. We were frightened by this complete silence and the absence of people, and desperate to find out what was happening.

József suggested that we should try and enter a house. We approached the gate of the nearest house, a small neat bungalow, and tried to ring the doorbell. There was no electricity and the doorbell didn't work, so we knocked on the gate, but to no avail. We walked along the street and knocked at the gate of almost every house. There was never any reply. All the houses in the street were small villas or bungalows usually occupied by one family. It seemed strange that out of the whole street, nobody answered the door. Were the houses empty? Where had all the people gone? Finally we noticed that the gate of one of the larger houses was slightly ajar. We opened the gate and entered the house, expecting to have to apologize for our intrusion, but there was no one there. The inside of the house was in complete disarray: in all the rooms the contents of the cupboards were spilled on to the tables and floor, as though the family had fled in a hurry, and someone had been searching for some valuables they might have left behind. In the kitchen the stove hadn't been used for some time and was completely cold. We tried to find something to eat and found a few cubes of sugar and some dry bread. We then went through the clothes on the floor, because all of us needed better shoes and warmer jackets and trousers. There was nothing suitable for the boys, but there were good boots for us girls and we chose some. We also found warm socks and good quality trousers and jackets, but again only women's clothes. It looked as though all the men's shoes, boots and clothes had been taken and there was nothing left. I changed into my new clothes: comfortable warm boots, brown corduroy trousers and a matching warm padded jacket. Not only did I feel quite warm, but thought that I was smartly dressed. When we finished, we left and tried to find warm things for the boys in other houses but there were no men's clothes to be found in any of them. (Only later did we find out why: the Russian soldiers had been through the houses and had taken everything they could use, such as menswear, but of course they left the women's clothes.) We were desperate to meet some living people and find out what was going on; the abandoned streets and houses made us feel very uncomfortable. Several other houses were open and in a similar state of disarray to the first one, with no people in them. What had happened to everyone, was there some sort of plague that had made all the people flee? Finally, we reached an apartment block. This building had a cellar that must have been previously used as an air-raid shelter. We tried to get into it but the door was locked. Nevertheless, our hopes were raised when we heard voices. We knocked at the door, and after a while someone asked, 'Who is there?' We explained that we had just left Budapest and were on our way to Szeged, but found it strange that there was no one about. Then we were asked whether there were any Russians with us. We were surprised by this question, but answered truthfully that there were no Russians with us, and finally someone opened the door. The cellar was packed full of people, and felt deliciously warm. When we asked why everyone was in the shelter and not in their houses, a middle-aged blonde woman answered that it was not safe to be outside, because the Russian soldiers raped all the women, young and old, and took the men away to be sent to Russia as prisoners of war. Apparently some of the genuine prisoners often escaped, and rather then trying to catch them, the Russian soldiers just took any man, young or old, and substituted him for the escapee. We listened to this news, in a state of disbelief. It seemed impossible that the heroic members of the Russian army would behave like this. Nevertheless, we thought we had better be cautious.

I spoke some Russian and was therefore appointed by our group to be the spokesperson in case we needed to negotiate with any Russian soldiers. We stayed in the shelter for a while, got some food and a hot drink, and thus fortified, set off on our way to Szeged.

The main road to Szolnok started on the periphery of Budapest. It had been cleared of snow so that Russian army trucks and vehicles could send supplies to, and communicate with, their fighting troops in Budapest. It was much easier walking along these main roads. Apart from the army vehicles carrying troops and supplies to Budapest and lorries returning south, there was no other traffic on the road. The flat snow-covered fields either side of the road and the eerie silence made us feel uncomfortable. Still, there were five of us, and we thought that we were in friendly territory, in spite of what we had just heard.

We had a few hours of daylight left and decided to walk as fast as we could. At dusk, we took a side road that led to a small village, where we hoped to find shelter for the night. We reached the village, but the situation there was no different from that we had found on the outskirts of Budapest. Empty streets, abandoned houses, and no one to be seen. We searched for food, but could find nothing until Lea shouted with delight: 'I've found a bag of flour, we could make something with it.' All five of us felt better already, and went to have a look at Lea's treasure. There were many saucepans scattered about in various kitchens so we took one and filled it with snow. Then we discovered some firewood in one of the sheds and lit a fire in the stove, ready to prepare something from the flour. When the snow in the saucepan melted we poured a little of what we thought was flour into the saucepan, but to our surprise the mixture became solid and smelled foul. It definitely wasn't flour, but what was it? Suddenly, András laughed and said: 'This is plaster of Paris – when I broke my wrist the mixture used to set it was the same as this.' Our disappointment was indescribable, but we were so exhausted that we just boiled some more water from melting snow, kept the fire going, found some blankets and went to sleep. We knew then that we would have to approach the Russian soldiers and ask them for food.

Next morning we set off again into the bitter cold and walked along the main road determined to acquire some food, for we were starving. The hunger exacerbated the feeling of cold. Our feet were ice-cold, and my toes hurt. Around midday we approached a small house by the roadside. We saw a group of five or six Russian soldiers carrying firewood. They looked rather shabby, and were of Asian origin. When talking to each other they used a language that was not Russian and which I couldn't understand or identify. Still, we hoped that this might be our chance to get some food. I approached the soldiers and asked them in my broken Russian whether they would give us some food. I spun a tale, partly true, that we were fleeing from the German soldiers to find safety in Russian occupied Hungary. I told them that I came from Slovakia and that my fiancé was a partisan fighting the Germans. One of the Russians asked who the others were, and they eyed the three boys with particular suspicion. I didn't mention that we were Jewish because I'd heard many stories about the anti-Semitic feelings of many Russians.

Finally, the Russians agreed to give us hot soup and bread if we would chop some wood for them and help them with heating up water for their bath. We were happy with the deal. The three boys in our group chopped the wood and Lea and I piled the chopped wood onto a wheelbarrow. When the wheelbarrow was full, József asked me to enquire where he should take it. The Russian soldier pointed at József and told me that he didn't want him to take the wood into the hut, but wanted me and Lea to do it. We were to bring the wheelbarrow into the hut and light a fire in the stove to heat the water for their bath. Neither of us liked the idea, and József just got hold of the wheelbarrow and took it into the hut. One of the other soldiers came out with dishes filled with hot soup and with some bread. We fell on the hot soup and consumed it in no time at all. After we had eaten, another of the soldiers tried to persuade Lea and I to go into the hut to light the fire. They promised us more food and some vodka, but I refused, pointing out that we were in a hurry. Just then a young woman with a boy of 4 or 5 passed by. At this point the Russians stopped being interested in us, got hold of the woman and child and pushed them into the hut. We heard terrible screams and sounds of a struggle. We were sure that the four soldiers were raping the woman. After about forty minutes, the woman and the child emerged from the hut. The child was crying and the woman looked badly bruised. Lea and I felt sorry for them, but we were also relieved that we had resisted the invitations to enter the hut.

After this traumatic episode we got quickly on our way. We had learned our lesson: we had to be very careful when dealing with our liberators. Though rape is not quite the same as being gassed it still is preferable to avoid it.

We walked on, in the hope that, as we got further away from the area newly liberated by the Russians, the situation would improve and the soldiers would be better behaved. The first signs of improvement became apparent when, after about an hour of walking on the icy road, we came across a convoy of army trucks travelling in the same direction as us. One of the trucks stopped and a tall good-looking Russian officer jumped down and asked us who we were and what we were doing on the road. I explained to him that we wanted to get away from the Germans and were on our way to Szeged. He smiled at me, and very chivalrously asked if we would accept some help. He offered to take us to a village about 40 km south of there and also told us that he would arrange for us to get some food. We were very tired and for some reason I trusted this man, so after a brief consultation we accepted the offer and climbed into the truck. By the time it got dark we arrived at a village, and the Russian soldier took us to an empty house where he said we could stay the night. He also gave us some firewood so we could light the fire and get warm. He then invited us to share their dinner and spend the evening with his unit. We were very grateful for the offer of food, and also relieved to meet some soldiers who behaved in a civilized manner. We went with the officer to the building where the soldiers had their dinner, and as soon as we entered, we heard the sound of a harmonica. There was singing, music and lively chatter. Everyone was very friendly. After the meal and a few glasses of vodka, some of the soldiers started to dance. The anticipation of the end of their fighting was all too obvious, but I was still filled with admiration at this display of joy in the face of so much hardship and suffering.

Next morning we thanked our hosts, said goodbye, and set out to continue our journey on foot. We felt quite strong after a good meal and a night's sleep in a warm house. The landscape was depressing though; flat as a pancake, covered in deep snow and with hardly any sign of life. We must have marched another 20 km and it was getting dark when we heard the barking of dogs, and knew that we were approaching a village. When we reached it, life seemed to be more or less normal there. The chimneys were smoking, the streets were cleared of snow and people were walking the streets.

We asked a peasant woman who was clearing the snow from outside the house where we were. In a friendly manner, she told us that we were quite close to Szolnok. When we asked about life under the Russian occupation, she said: 'After the first plunder and rape, a different group of Russian soldiers came to occupy us. They're still here, and they are well behaved, helpful and keen to help us get back to normal life. So we are living like before, and don't take much notice of the Russians. They leave us alone too.' I asked what her name was, she said it was Anna. We too introduced ourselves. Anna asked us where we came from, and was surprised that we had dared to walk on foot from Budapest. She offered to give us some food and allow us to sleep in the stables with the cows. We were very grateful to her and after some bread and cheese in the farmhouse kitchen we retreated to the stables. It was quite warm in there, and the smell didn't prevent any of us from falling asleep after our tiring walk.

After this, our journey to Szeged became easier; we often hitched lifts from the Russian soldiers who drove their trucks along the road, and in most villages we were helped and given food and shelter. About a week after we had set out on our journey, we arrived at Szeged.

LIFE IN SZEGED

As soon as we arrived in Szeged, we noticed that life seemed quite normal there. The snow was cleared from the pavements, the streets were full of people who were well wrapped up and wore felt boots. The shops were selling all sorts of interesting goods, though we were only interested in the food stores; we were hungry all the time, but had no money to buy anything.

We had to find out whether there were any remnants of the Jewish community left, or any organization that would help Jewish refugees returning from various parts of liberated Europe. We thought the most likely place for an office dealing with these matters would be around the synagogue, so we asked one of the people on the street to point us in the right direction. The synagogue in Szeged is an impressive building, with a colourfully tiled roof and a hint of Moorish style. It is situated in a tree-lined street, but in the middle of this cold winter the trees were barren and the street was unattractive and shabby. We soon discovered that next to the synagogue there was a house that belonged to the Jewish community. On the gate of this house there was a notice pointing to an office that supposedly dealt with returning Jews from liberated Europe. We were delighted to have found the right place. We walked to the office and entered a poorly furnished room. It seemed that we were the only 'clients'. Three or four young people manned the office and sat behind old desks. They were pleased to see us, and asked where we came from, and what we wanted to do. We explained to them that we had walked from Budapest to Szeged, and told them about our activities in Budapest and the ties we had with the Zionists in Budapest, helping to forge documents and trying to rescue Jews. One of the young men in the office, Ernest, knew of József's activities, and he suggested that we should stay here in Szeged and help with the work in the office. Ernest explained that the office had been set up by a left-wing Zionist youth group called Hashomer Hazair. Its role was to help Jews who were returning from all parts of Europe to emigrate to Palestine through Cyprus, by supplying them with travel documents and money. Jewish agencies committed to establishing a Jewish state in Palestine financed this office and its efforts, at least in part. Another of their activities was to prepare young people for life in a kibbutz in Palestine. This meant getting used to living in a community with other people, working together and sharing everything.

All five of us agreed that we would like to stay and help with this effort. At the same time we were also looking forward to living with other young people and exploring what life in a kibbutz might be like.

We were taken to an apartment in the same building, with a kitchen, bathroom and several rooms that had been converted into dormitories, with beds and some cupboards. There were about five or six beds in each room. I was in a room with Lea and three other girls, and the boys were in separate rooms. We had very few possessions and it didn't take long to put them away. We compared each other's coats and dresses and liked the idea of sharing them. There was also a lounge with enough room for all of us to get together.

This is how my strange life as a Zionist recruiting officer started. I myself toyed with the idea of emigrating to Palestine for some time, but was never quite sure about the correctness of the Zionist ideology, or whether I could settle outside Europe. In spite of all my terrible experiences, I felt I belonged in Europe.

Every morning we were woken by a loudspeaker piping cheerful music through all the rooms. Then those of us who were on duty to prepare breakfast went to the kitchen, and the others performed various tasks assigned to them. Most mornings were spent with these mundane chores.

Those of us who worked in the office met survivors returning from work camps and concentration camps, or who were hiding, or fighting with partisan groups. Every person had a special story to tell, and for us it was a distressing experience to hear of so much suffering.

Later in the afternoon we all gathered in the lounge and were given political education: lectures about the history of Palestine, and the ideology of Zionism. We discussed articles written by Theodor Herzl, Chaim Weizmann and other influential figures in the Zionist movement. Since our group was a socialist branch, we shared all our possessions, and had little privacy. For the first few weeks the novelty of this life fascinated me, and I quite enjoyed it. I also relished the abundance of food. I used to go to the market where peasant women were selling exquisite poppy seed cakes and cheese strudel, and gorge myself with them. Nevertheless, after a while I felt more and more disillusioned with this life, with the indoctrination we received and with the almost military drill and monotony of our life, which was difficult to tolerate.

I needed some distraction, some more contact with real life outside our commune, and also some more intellectual challenges. I was hungry to learn things in a more structured way. Having been deprived of formal education for so long, I longed to make up for it.

Szeged had a good university, and I believed that enrolling as a student and attending some lectures might help me. I wasn't sure whether I would be accepted because I had had no secondary school education, but I tried nevertheless and was accepted to attend a course in history and literature. The term started in March and it was only February, so I had a few weeks to wait.

I was undecided about my future and wanted to rethink everything that I so readily accepted when I first arrived in Szeged. I had now been there for over a month and during this time I had had no news about my relatives in Budapest, my father in the work camp, my mother in the concentration camp, or any family members or friends, who might have been liberated and returned to Budapest. I decided that it was time to find out more about my family. First I would visit my aunt in Budapest. I arranged to get some time off, and prepared for my journey. I knew that there was a great shortage of food in Budapest and so I went to the market and bought lots of sausages, salami and other things that would survive the journey, for I anticipated that it would take me at least three days to get there.

VISIT TO BUDAPEST

I packed all the food and some of my things into a rucksack and started on my journey. It was the end of February and some trains were running, though most of them were local. The fastest and most efficient ones were reserved for Russian officers and army personnel. With my reasonable knowledge of Russian I was confident that I might get a ride in one of those trains. Szeged station was only a short walk from where we stayed. Lea accompanied me to help with my luggage. This was the first time we had been alone for a long time. I asked her how she liked living in a 'kibbutz' type environment. She said she loved it and talked with great enthusiasm about emigrating to Palestine, where she wanted to help to build a new home for Jews. I didn't tell her about my doubts, for I was not sure myself as to what I really felt or wanted. Above all it was the nationalistic flavour of the Zionist movement that worried me, as did the fact that Palestine was in the Middle East, a place so different from central Europe. But I had not yet clarified my views on the subject. I knew that I had to distance myself from it all and to think about my future.

The station was very busy: full of civilians like me and Russian soldiers. Although there were several trains waiting, no one knew anything about their destination. There was complete chaos, with people running in all directions, trying to get some information.

Having said goodbye to Lea, I saw that there were some Russian soldiers in one of the trains. I asked them where they were heading, and to my delight they said 'Budapest'. I told them that I would like to visit my relatives in Budapest and bring them some food. I didn't even have to ask, because one of the officers said that I could join them and travel with them all the way to Budapest. He was a gentle looking person who introduced himself as Pjotr, and I trusted him immediately. I felt quite safe with him. After quite a long wait, the train started to move. It made slow progress to Szolnok. Then we were told that we would have to change trains, because there was some problem with our train. So we got out, and went to the waiting room. It was then that I noticed that my 'protector' carried a violin case. I asked him whether it was his violin and whether he played it. He replied that if we had to wait a long time, he would play his violin for us all. As it turned out, we had to wait all night and had plenty of time to listen to Pjotr playing the violin. Finally, he stopped playing and began to talk to me. He asked where I came from, and about my family. I told him that I was Jewish, and that I didn't know what had happened to my parents. Pjotr listened with great concentration and when I had finished he told me not to tell any Russian soldier that I was Jewish. It was mainly Ukrainians who occupied this part of Hungary and most of the soldiers were anti-Semitic. Pjotr too was a Jew, but no one knew about it. I was not entirely surprised by these revelations, for I had guessed from some of the remarks made by the Russian soldiers I had came across that the Jews were none too popular. My 'protector' then gave me some bread and cheese and a drink of vodka to keep me warm, which was most welcome, for the waiting room was freezing cold.

We resumed our journey in the morning, when we boarded another train. This train was to take us all the way to Budapest, where we arrived in the evening.

On stepping out of the railway station, I noticed that the streets of Budapest were empty, and just as shabby as before I had left. Pjotr insisted he take me to my aunt's house, for according to his information the streets of Budapest were not entirely safe. My Aunt Manci's apartment was not too far from the station and I reached there safely under Pjotr's protection. It was with some regret that I said goodbye to him.

I entered the house and found the lift. The apartment was on the fifth floor, and I wondered whether the lift was working. The metal door to the lift opened easily, and the inside was clean, the wood panelled walls polished, so with any luck it would work. I pressed the button for the fifth floor and amazingly the lift moved. I rang the doorbell to my aunt's apartment and that too worked. After a while, she opened the door. As always, the reunion was a pleasurable experience and this time even more so, for we were both aware that it was only by some miracle that we had survived. The people who had occupied the apartment during the siege of Budapest, when I had last visited, had all moved out so that now it was like old times – only Manci and her husband Andor were there. It was cold in the apartment, but the warm welcome I received counteracted this. Manci led me into the sitting-room, which was impeccable, with the furniture and the parquet floors polished and the carpets cleaned. I was desperate for news about the family, and what I heard was not altogether good.

Although my Aunt Ada and her husband Arthur had survived and returned from hiding, my father had not been seen since his last visit to my aunt in November, just before I arrived in Budapest. Though his unit in the work camp might have been moved further west it was very worrying that we had not heard from him. There was no news about my mother either. Still, the war was not over yet, so there was still hope that she may be alive. My other relatives in Budapest were safe. My cousin Baby and her family were back in their house and I was looking forward to seeing them.

Life in Budapest was hard. There was a shortage of food, fuel for heating the houses was also in short supply and walking the streets was still risky. There was no public transport and only one bridge connected Pest with Buda. The food I brought with me was much appreciated. Now we had sausages and salami, but there was no bread. Apparently it was possible to buy some bread at the bakery on Szt. István körút, quite close by. My aunt and I put on warm clothes – I was lent a big fur hat – and went out. There was a long queue in front of the shop that sold bread and we joined it. The queue was a good sign for it seemed likely that there would be some bread at the end of it. It was bitterly cold, so we were glad of our warm clothes. We passed the time talking to each other. I told my aunt about my job in Szeged with the Zionist agency, about my life in the commune and about my doubts whether emigration to Palestine would be a suitable option for me. Manci didn't interrupt me and said very little.

While we were talking, a group of Russian soldiers came along moved right to the front of the queue and entered the shop. 'They always do this,' said my aunt, 'and then there is no bread left for the people in the queue.' Nevertheless, we continued to wait. It was the right decision, for we managed to get a loaf of bread, even though we were among the last people. Almost immediately, the shop closed and the notice 'No more bread' was displayed on the door. I was carrying the loaf under my arm, when a scruffy looking soldier approached, grabbed the bread from under my arm and got hold of my hand. '*Davay, poyd suda*' (Come on, come here) he shouted. He tried to drag me along with him, hoping that I would follow him because he had the bread. My aunt was truly alarmed; she got hold of my arm and tried to pull me away from the soldier. My aunt's Russian was better then mine, and she screamed at him: 'Let go of her, keep the bread.' The soldier was so surprised at being spoken to in Russian that he loosened his grip on my hand for just long enough for me to pull away. Together with my aunt I started to run. Perhaps the soldier was content with the bread; anyway he didn't follow us. Thus all our efforts to get some bread were in vain, but we were pleased to get home safely without any further adventures. I think my aunt was more alarmed then I was, for apparently rape and violence were still rampant on the streets of Budapest.

Back in the apartment, Andor was waiting, and was disappointed that we came back empty-handed. Obviously, there was no hope for bread any more that day. May be there would be some bread on sale the next day, when we would have to join the queue at dawn. My aunt, always positive, suggested:

'Let's just have some sausage and cheese – we don't have to have bread with it.' She boiled some water, put some substitute coffee powder into it and we settled around the kitchen table to eat. Both Manci and Andor must have been starving, the food disappeared so quickly. Then we went into the sitting room. I sat in a chair facing an oil painting I knew and liked so well. It was a landscape typical of northern Hungary and southern Slovakia, a meadow in a valley and a small hill with trees in the background. A young woman dressed in a long flowing skirt and white blouse was standing in the meadow looking towards the hill, as if waiting for someone to come. The painting was well cared for, but in the left-hand corner there was a hole surrounded by slightly blackened edges. 'How did this hole get here?' I asked, 'Did someone deliberately damage the picture?' 'Oh no,' my uncle Andor said, 'during the street fighting between the Germans and Russians, a stray bullet shattered the window and hit the picture. Manci and I were sitting here reading when it happened, and were glad the bullet only hit the picture and no one was injured.' What my uncle said was true of course, but all the same, I thought that by hitting the picture the bullet had symbolically damaged something important, some memories that would be changed for ever.

I stayed in Budapest a few more days, and talked to Manci about the future. She agreed with my doubts about emigration to Palestine, and said that I should not take any decisions just yet, or make any plans for the future. She reminded me rightly that my decision concerned not only me, but also all those who love me. There was still hope that my mother and father were alive and might return and then our future as a family had to be considered. She urged me not to rush into anything and to wait until the war was properly over, when we would know more about the fate of family members. I was grateful to her for her advice.

BACK IN SZEGED

My return to Szeged was uneventful. I was upset that there had been no news of my father but I still hoped that he might return. Being away from Budapest helped me to wait and hope. It was good to be back in Szeged; everything was much more peaceful there, and my friends were understanding and supportive. The routine was now welcome. In fact I became so content that I put on a lot of weight. So, no more poppy-seed cakes for me from the market, or cheese strudel from the nearby shop: I couldn't afford a new set of clothes. I attended a few lectures at the University, and enjoyed them very much. But there wasn't enough time to settle down and become a serious student.

In May the official end of the war with Germany was finally declared with the total surrender of Nazi Germany. We were jubilant, for this meant freedom and more importantly, a new start to our lives. It also meant that the waiting was over and we could start to search seriously for our families. Most of us who had lived together for the past few months decided to return to our various hometowns to find out who had survived. Saying goodbye to each other, it was hard to accept that our life together had finished; yet we knew that each of us would have to make our own decisions as to what to do with our lives now. Before parting we promised that we would try to keep in touch, though deep down we were aware that these vows were made mainly to make the parting less painful, and that we might not see each other again.

RETURN HOME

There were some regular trains now running from Szeged to Budapest, but these were very crowded. Nevertheless I managed to squeeze into one, and stood for the whole nine hour journey. My body and limbs were stiff when I arrived in Budapest, and made my way to Aunt Manci's. As usual, I was warmly received. My first question of course was whether there was any news from my parents, but Manci had not heard anything. We went to a makeshift office at the Jewish community centre to look at the names of people who had returned from camps. The walls of an entire room were covered with names and addresses, but we found nothing about my parents. Manci and I wrote our name and address down on a piece of paper and pinned it to the wall. I returned to the apartment troubled and disappointed; I thought that my father ought to have been back from his work camp, which had still been in Hungary in November. Despite my disappointment, I still hoped that my parents might return.

Manci arranged a family gathering to discuss my future. After all, I was only 18 and seemingly an orphan. My family wanted to take care of me, and my uncles and aunts tried to persuade me to stay with them in Budapest, and not return home to Czechoslovakia. They would look after me at least until I knew what had happened to my parents. The offer was tempting, but I wanted to go back to Trnava to be there when my parents came back. After several hours of discussion, my aunts and uncles reluctantly agreed to let me leave Budapest and go home.

In an office set up to deal with refugees that were returning home, I got my identity documents and for the first time in many months I became officially myself again – Gerti Sidon. It felt good to retrieve my identity and have it all written down on paper. Armed with these documents I set off on my own, now quite legally, by train to Trnava.

It was the end of May, and spring was well advanced. The fields were a lush green, and in the meadows thousands of bluebells decorated the grass. I was enchanted by the beauty of the countryside, and delighted to be back. Above all, I was full of hope that my parents would come home and that we would be reunited. After all, not so long ago, father had been alive and well and my mother had been sent to camp when the war was almost over – she might have survived.

I arrived in Trnava late in the afternoon and went straight

to what used to be our house. The house still stood there as though nothing had changed. I went up the flight of stairs where our flat used to be and rang the bell. Mr Simončič, our former shop assistant, appeared at the door and gazed at me in horror: 'Oh God,' he exclaimed, 'you are still alive.' I didn't reply, but brushed passed him and entered our home. Marushka was settled in what used to be my room, but when she saw me she disappeared without a word.

What was I to do? I needed some time to ascertain whether my parents or any relatives in Slovakia had returned, and I had nowhere else to go.

Trnava was still under Russians occupation, and there was an office that dealt with people returning from Nazi persecution to their homes. I went to the office and explained my position. I was told that I should live in my old home, which would be returned to my family. After completing some paperwork, a Russian officer accompanied me to the house, made sure that I should be given my bedroom immediately and explained to Mr Simončič that the house should be returned to me. Mr Simončič and his family were given a deadline to vacate the premises.

As soon as I could I started to search for my parents. I visited various offices similar to the one in Budapest where returning refugees left their names and addresses pinned to the wall, and searched for hours for a familiar name. There were also lists published by the Red Cross and various organizations that dealt with survivors of the holocaust, but I did not find my mother's or father's name anywhere. For about six weeks I continued my search and each day that passed took away some hope.

My mother's sister Kornelia survived and she too was searching for her two daughters who had been sent to a concentration camp. She was lucky, for one day they turned up in Trnava.

After six weeks of searching and hoping, I had to make a decision.

Walter and my friend Inge survived, and together we

discussed our future. All three of us wanted to study. However, since neither of us had completed our secondary school education we had to do that first. We discovered that the Department of Education of the Czechoslovak Republic had set up courses to help those who missed out on their education due to Nazi persecution, to enable them to complete their education during the summer of 1945. The course available to us was in Bratislava, and we enrolled to attend this two month course.

What to do with the house in Trnava that had now been returned to me? I didn't want it without my parents there, and vowed never to return. I wanted to get rid of it quickly, so I sold it for a golden watch, a Leica camera and a typewriter. Without any ties to home, I was free to start my new life, and after completing the course in Bratislava, Inge, Walter and I moved to Prague to start our university studies.

Epilogue

Having put so much effort into surviving the war and avoiding being slaughtered in the Nazi death camps, I had a problem: what do I do with the rest of my life? I wanted to be a writer or a film director, but I was afraid that I was not good enough to suceed at either of these professions. I was also concerned about my financial situation and was aware that I needed a profession that would enable me to make a reasonable living. Finally, I opted for medicine. It is a profession where it is possible to do quite a bit for other people and to be a useful member of the community, and I could always keep my options open. After all, Chekhov and many great writers were medical doctors, as well as writers. Walter and Inge decided to study chemical engineering and we all went to Prague to embark on our studies.

Walter and I got married while we were still students. We lived in a small apartment and enjoyed our new life. We both worked hard and felt privileged to be able to study. Shortly after I qualified as a medical doctor, our first daughter Helena was born, and two years later our second child Zuzana. I never thought it possible to be so happy: to give birth and nurture my babies made me feel that our families continued in spite of all the odds. I guess every young woman who survived the holocaust and saw her family perish must have felt the same.

At the same time my career started to take shape. While I was still a medical student, my interests focused on research. I enjoyed the work, and found the fact that it required imagination exciting. I still wanted to work with patients, however, and after I qualified I got a job at the Department of Neurology at the medical school. There I learned how to diagnose patients with neurological disorders, and in terms of puzzle solving this was very interesting. Nevertheless it was disturbing that once the puzzle was solved and the diagnosis established, there was little one could do for the patient. This for me was very frustrating, so I went back to research, ended up as a researcher in neuroscience and started work on my PhD.

This was an interesting period not only for me personally, but also for Czechoslovak science. During Nazi occupation, Czechoslovak science was more or less destroyed; the universities were closed and possibilities for research did not exist. Ours was the first 'generation' after the war to try to establish a flourishing scientific field. What we lacked in know-how and facilities we compensated for by enthusiasm. Soon new scientific institutes were established, where the atmosphere provided an excellent breeding ground for creative thought and imagination.

I worked in the Institute of Physiology at the Czechoslovak Academy of Science and tried to combine hard work with family life, unsuccessfully, as it turned out. My relationship with Walter deteriorated and we separated, which was painful for both of us. We tried to share our responsibilities for the children as best we could but it was very hard.

These difficulties within our family took place during the time when our idealistic optimism about building a new, just, socialist society was squashed by political events that seemed to us unbelievable. After the war many young people, myself included, believed that communism was the solution to many of the social problems we had witnessed before and during the war. We also looked towards the Soviet Union as our staunchest ally, for after the disappointment in 1938 of the Munich agreement between Hitler, Britain and France when our country was betrayed and handed over to Hitler, we had no faith in Western democracy. Thus we rallied with great enthusiasm for communism. Then, when with our support the communists took charge of our country, I started to

177

become aware of our mistake and of the true nature of that government. Our disillusion started when one of the most popular political leaders, Jan Masaryk, was murdered (though it was presented to us as suicide). Shortly afterwards the political trials that branded the most prominent and trusted representatives of the new communist governments as traitors started and ended with the execution of eleven members of the Communist Party. In spite of this evidence that we were dealing with an evil system, we struggled to hold on to our convictions and hoped that things would improve. We were helped in our optimism by the atmosphere at work and the success we had at building up scientific research within the Institute.

Our scientific endeavour made us increasingly aware that we were part of an international scientific community where many colleagues from all parts of the world shared interests similar to ours, and worked hard on solving the same problems. We had a passionate desire to communicate with our colleagues from all over the world and discuss our scientific ideas with theirs, yet we felt isolated from this community. Gradually, however we started to make contact. I was attending scientific meetings in Russia, Poland, Hungary, England and France, and I became aware of the tremendous possibilities for reaching out towards new horizons through these new contacts.

Meanwhile I was struggling to bring up my two daughters. There were serious shortages of food, long queues for essential articles and some rationing, but somehow none of these difficulties seemed to dampen my lust for knowledge and life.

It was during this time that my colleague invited an English scientist to help her to introduce some new methods in our Institute. As a reward for his help, she took him skiing to the mountains, but she then had to return unexpectedly to Prague. She asked me whether I could go to the mountains to take over looking after her English visitor and show him around. It was only for two days, and I was able to make arrangements so that I could help out.

178

Maybe it was the magic of the mountains, the awkwardness of being with someone with whom it was out of the question to have a permanent relationship (for at that time, at the height of the cold war, it was impossible to marry or live with a partner from a capitalist country) that lifted all our inhibitions. Whatever the reason, quite irresponsibly we fell madly in love.

Over the next two years we met as often as we could. 'My Englishman' took a sabbatical to go and work in Poland, where I could get permission to travel and meet up with him. We also met on the Polish–Slovak border in the Tatra Mountains. Finally we decided that we could not carry on like this and would like to live together permanently. It was 1958, two years after the Russians squashed the Hungarian uprising and it was unthinkable that my children and I would be allowed to emigrate to England. Neither was it possible for my Englishman to come and live in Czechoslovakia. So I tried to escape from Czechoslovakia. I applied for holidays in Yugoslavia and East Germany, from where it might be possible to escape. But the Czechoslovak secret police knew about my relationship, and I did not get permission to go anywhere together with my children. I was however allowed to travel without them, for it was clear that I would never leave without them.

My wartime experience of crossing borders illegally and defying authority helped me not to give up hope, for I believed that nothing is quite as impossible as it seems. And again this turned out to be true.

Finally I got a break: I was invited to attend a meeting in Poland and got a passport with an exit visa stamped in it that stated: 'To Poland and back through any country in Europe'. I thought it was possible to take advantage of this wording, but there were several obstacles I had to overcome. My daughters were not included in my passport and I could not bring them with me to Poland. I travelled to Poland alone, and left my children with a child minder. After I had arrived in Poland, I sent a cable to my English friend and asked him to send an air ticket for me and the two children for travelling from Warsaw to Prague via Copenhagen. The tickets arrived with a cable 'You have all my love'. Now I had to bring the children to Warsaw, get a Danish transit visa and enter my children's names into my passport. Quite a task!

I could not return to Prague legally for my passport would have been taken away from me, so I had to cross the Polish–Czech border illegally. I knew the mountains quite well, so I was confident that I could accomplish this. Then I had to bring my daughters aged 4 and 6 back with me across the same border. For our crossing, I chose a place in the Giant Mountains where there was a chair lift that went to the top of a mountain called Snežka from the Czech side of the mountain range. On the Polish side the way was mainly downhill, but it was still a six hour walk to the nearest railway station. I was worried that I could not accomplish this by myself and was therefore delighted when a Polish friend of mine offered to help me. He suggested that he wait for us at a certain agreed spot for two days running on the Polish side of the border and help me and the children to reach the next railway station. I am to this day grateful to him for this, for without his help I could not have managed to get to the train before dark.

Thus, with these preparations completed, I set off, crossed the border, arrived in Prague in the evening and went to our home, where my children were waiting for me. I told them that the next morning we were going for a trip to the mountains. That night, my last in my old home, I didn't sleep much. In the early morning my two daughters and I set off with a backpack each to catch a bus to the mountains. We left all our things in Prague, all my efforts to build up a home had come to nothing. But I didn't think about any of this, neither did I allow myself to think of the risk that I was taking. After all, if I had failed and been caught by the police, I would have been put in prison, and what would have happened to my children? With hindsight, I should never have taken such risks.

The three of us crossed the Czechoslovak–Polish border

without difficulties. My Polish friend was waiting for us at the top of the mountain on the Polish side and helped me to carry the children and reach the railway station, where we boarded a train for Warsaw. In Warsaw we stayed overnight in a friend's house. The next day I entered my daughters' names into my passport and, equipped with this forged document, I went to the Danish embassy to apply for a twenty-four-hour transit visa, to stop in Copenhagen on our way from Warsaw to Prague. Miraculously, I had no difficulty obtaining this transit visa. Equipped with my forged passport and the transit visa we boarded an SAS plane to Copenhagen. We arrived in Copenhagen and my English friend with his Danish friend were waiting for us there. From then on, things seemed to go smoothly. I got a job in Denmark and stayed there for a while. Finally we got married and moved to London.

It was difficult to settle in a new place with hardly any friends, and I was desperately homesick for Prague. Getting a job in England for a foreign woman with two young children and pregnant with another child was hard as well. Without the help of some of my colleagues, who had confidence in my work and abilities, it would have been impossible to get a job, and research for me had become an essential part of life.

I had two more children by my second husband, and their arrival helped me to make a start and enjoy my life in England. After a few years in England I felt quite settled. My second marriage didn't last either, but that in a way was not surprising. There were too many problems; my attachment to my children from my first marriage was not tolerated by my husband, and finally it seemed best to separate.

The children grew up too fast and now I regret that I did not spend more time with them. The next generation, my grandchildren, are an immense source of pleasure.

I get a lot of satisfaction from my research, and I was successful enough to become a university professor. Maybe my training during the war, when I had to use my imagination and often defy authority, helped me to come up with unconventional ideas in my research.

The Library of Holocaust Testimonies

Through Blood and Tears:
Surviving Hitler and Stalin
Henry Skorr

Henry Skorr has told his story, in a series of interviews conducted by Ivan Sokolov, in an effort to preserve the memory of those he loved, and a world that no longer exists. Henry takes the reader from his childhood in Kalisz, Poland, through the horrors of the Nazi occupation, the insanity and brutality of the Soviet system, the corruption of the newly re-formed Poland, and finally to the shores of Israel. The main part of the story deals with his time in the Soviet Union, providing the reader with a rare insight into the plight of Polish-Jewish refugees, as well as native Russians, during the war years. The memoir adds an important voice to the catalogue of survivors' tales; with courage and honesty, Henry Skorr articulately presents us with the Soviet experience, giving voice to the thousands who fled east and the millions he found there.

February 2006, 384 pages
ISBN 0 85303 477 X

The Library of Holocaust Testimonies

Scorched
Irit Amiel
Translated from the Hebrew by Riva Rubin

The heroes of the stories in this book are people who in the hell of the Holocaust were doomed for life, people who cannot or do not want to speak about their past, about the heavy baggage of their life's experiences. Being a witness, Irit Amiel translates the long silence of people living in the Israeli melting pot into testimony. The stories are written in a simple and restrained way, but the voices coming out touch the most profound human feelings. These miniature proses achieve a weight through the use of poetic shortcuts, such as the two-page memory about the last parting from home and parents. 'I was then eleven years old and from that very moment I have never felt at home in life again.'

June 2006, 94 pages
ISBN 0 85303 634 9

The Library of Holocaust Testimonies

A Village Named Dowgalishok: The Massacre at Radun and Eishishok
Avraham Aviel

This is the authentic and unique story of a young boy, skilfully describing the small Jewish agricultural village of Dowgalishok in eastern Poland (nowadays Byelorussia) and its neighbouring little towns Radun and Eishishok. With a tender loving touch the Jewish atmosphere is brought to life along with the village inhabitants, right from the pastoral days before the Second World War up to the sudden cruel and complete devastation under the Nazi regime.

The first part of the book is a vivid description of Yiddish-kite that has vanished forever. The second part is a shivering testimony of a survivor of the ghetto and the slaughter beside the terrible pit. The third and last part of the book is the story of twenty-two months of escape and struggle for life, first in the woods among farmers and later on as a partisan in the huge ancient forest.

The author tells his story in a simple, honest and fluent style, thus creating both a personal and a historical document. The book was highly appreciated by many critics, both in Israel and around the world for its moving and engulfing quality as well as for its documental value as a record from one of the darkest chapters of mankind.

June 2006, 300 pages
ISBN 0 85303 583 0

The Library of Holocaust Testimonies

My Own Vineyard
Miriam Akavia

This is a novel telling the story of three generations living in Krakow, Poland, from the beginning of the twentieth century to the German occupation of Poland in September 1939. The story of this large, middle-class Jewish family is also the story of a deeply rooted Jewish community and its considerable cultural and material achievements, until disaster strikes and it is wiped off the face of the earth.

June 2006, 350 pages
ISBN 0 85303 514 8

The Library of Holocaust Testimonies

Hiding in the Open:
A Young Fugitive in Nazi-Occupied Poland
Zenon Neumark

This is the story of Zenon Neumark's experiences as a Jewish teenager in Nazi-occupied Europe. He escaped from a forced labour camp in Tomaszow Mazowiecki, Poland, and lived under a false Polish Catholic identity, first in Warsaw and later in Vienna. It is a story about betrayal by friends and rescue by strangers; about a constant fear of being recognized as a Jew; the struggle for lodgings, work and blending in with the local population; a story of a double life working for opposing Resistance groups and opportunities to help others survive. The story ends with his recapture in the Warsaw Uprising of 1944 and deportation to a camp in Vienna, where, after another escape, he was liberated by the Soviet Army.

September 2006, 216 pages
ISBN 0 85303 633 0

The Library of Holocaust Testimonies

In the Shadow of Destruction:
Recollections of Transnistria
and Illegal Immigration to Eretz Israel,
1941–1947
Josef Govrin

Translated from the Hebrew original, *Be-Tzel ha-Avadon*, published by Beit Lohamei Haghetaot Press, 1999, in collaboration with Yad Vashem, Jerusalem, and the Center of Research of Romanian Jewry, the Hebrew University of Jerusalem.

This book is a personal account of a young boy's struggle to survive the Holocaust in Transnistria. The descriptions are presented against the background of contemporary events, combining personal recollections with an historic overview, before, during and after the Holocaust.

September 2006, 116 pages
ISBN 0 85303 643 8

The Library of Holocaust Testimonies

Sentenced to Life: The Story of a Survivor of the Lahwah Ghetto
Kopel Kolpanitzky
Translated from the Hebrew by Zvi Shulman

Kopel Kolpanitzky grew up in Lahwah, Byelorussia. His entire family was murdered in the Lahwah ghetto uprising against the Nazis, except for his father, who had previously been imprisoned by the Soviets. Living in the forests, he joined a partisan unit and then fought as a soldier in the Red Army. After the war he left the army and in trying to reach Eretz Yisrael almost reached the shores of Palestine before the ship he was on was stopped by the British and its passengers sent to a camp in Cyprus. A year later he finally arrived in Eretz Yisrajust before Israel's independence. He served in the Israel Defence Forces and later entered into business with his father, who had joined him in Israel in the early 1950s.

September 2006, 288 pages
ISBN 0 85303 695 0

1 Gerti, Prague, 1946

2 Gerti's parents (Josefine and Max), photograph taken at their engagement, 1922

3 Gerti's parents' engagement party, 1922. Front row (left to right): Gerti's parents Max and Josefine, Josefine's brother Feri. Second row (left to right): Gerti's two aunts and maternal grandmother Helena, uncle Arthur, uncle Arthur's wife Ada, grandfather Herman Frank, aunt Jetti. Third row (left to right): husbands of Gerti's two aunts, uncle Arnold's wife Terka, uncle Arnold, unknown man, aunt Kornelia's husband Lajos, aunt Kornelia, Jetti's husband Ferdinand

4 Aunt Manci (left) with Gerti's grandmother Jeanette, 1920

5 Snapshot taken in Luhačovice (a Moravian spa), 1932. Left to right: Gerti, cousin Julius on donkey, cousins Ilona, Elizabeth and Klari, unknown woman

6 Snapshot taken at the swimming pool of the sugar factory in Trnava, 1933. Front row (left to right): friend of the family (name unknown), Gerti, cousin Margaret, Gerti's paternal aunt Olga. Second row (left to right): Gerti's mother Josefine, Olga's husband Hans

7 Gerti, Prague, 1946

8 Gerti with fiancé Walter (Rudo Vrba), Prague, 1947

9 Snapshot of Gerti (middle) and friends Eva (left) and Inge
(right), Prague, 1947

10 Snapshot, Prague, 1948. Left to right: Walter, Eva, Anton
(Walter's friend and Eva's fiancé), Gerti

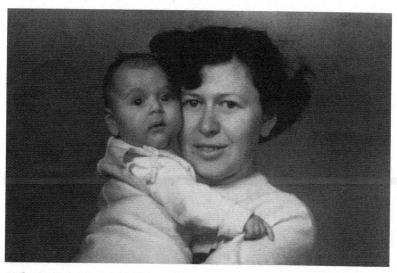

11 Gerti with her first child, Helena, 1952

12 Walter, Helena and Gerti, Prague Dejvice, 1955

13 Helena, Gerti and her second child, Zuza, Hungary, 1957